JOSEPH W. WALKER III

Date with *Destiny*

Find the Love You Need

Abingdon Press / *Nashville*

DATE WITH DESTINY
FIND THE LOVE YOU NEED

Copyright © 2011 by Abingdon Press

All rights reserved.

No part of this work may be reproduced or transmitted in any form or by any means, electronic or mechanical, including photocopying and recording, or by any information storage or retrieval system, except as may be expressly permitted by the 1976 Copyright Act or in writing from the publisher. Requests for permission should be addressed to Abingdon Press, P.O. Box 801, 201 Eighth Avenue South, Nashville, TN 37202-0801 or permissions@umpublishing.org.

This book is printed on acid-free paper.

Library of Congress Cataloging-in-Publication Data

Walker, Joseph Warren, 1967–
  Date with destiny : find the love you need / Joseph W. Walker III.
     p. cm.
  ISBN 978-1-4267-1246-3 (binding: pbk. : alk. paper)
  1. Interpersonal relations—Religious aspects—Christianity. 2.
Love—Religious aspects—Christianity. 3. Spirituality. I. Title.
  BV4597.52.W35 2011
  248.8'44—dc22

                                                                    2010043383

All scripture quotations are taken from the King James or Authorized Version of the Bible.

11 12 13 14 15 16 17 18 19 20—10 9 8 7 6 5 4 3 2 1

MANUFACTURED IN THE UNITED STATES OF AMERICA

CONTENTS

INTRODUCTION

I have had an opportunity to counsel and converse with thousands of folks who are frustrated. There is a common denominator in their relationships: they struggle with a lack of direction. They ask, "Where is this going? Where am I going? Where are we supposed to go?" So often the tension in many of their relationships is a result of competing agendas. I've seen good people who have struggled to make relationships work; but if you don't know the purpose of a thing, you will abuse it. If you don't know how a thing is supposed to end up, you will never be able to identify threats along the way. You will never be able to see the gifts along the way, either. And I am amazed at the number of people I encounter who have yet to connect with their God-given purpose, even with the numerous books, articles, and workshops dedicated to helping people find just that. For me purpose is the path toward destiny, and when I say destiny, I am referring to the way your life ends up—both as an individual and as a couple. God has a preordained destiny for us all; however, you will never arrive there if you do not have a clear understanding of your purpose.

This book is written to shed light on the power of purpose in relationships for couples. Why does God bring us together? Is there a purpose bigger than us? To these questions, I would argue, YES! When two people understand their purpose in life, it becomes a qualifier for healthy relationships. God merges their individual purposes so that they complement, not compete with each other.

God has blessed my wife, Stephaine, and me to pursue our destiny together. We are blessed to understand our purpose for being together. Our life is not without its challenges, but we are motivated by what we know is possible. Our relationship as a couple is bigger than either of us individually.

Relationships should never be self-serving. We must approach them selflessly, knowing that there is a larger purpose why God has brought us together. Both persons within the relationship support and motivate each other toward the attainment of their destiny. Our date is truly with destiny.

CHAPTER ONE

A DATE WITH DESTINY: ANTICIPATE GREATNESS

THE GREATNESS OF GOD

God has placed the promise of greatness inside of you. God has placed greatness inside of you as a couple. God will meet you wherever you are, despite wherever you've been. Seize this promise. Accept your gift. Align yourselves with God's purpose, and begin your date with destiny.

One of the most important lessons that every believer needs to know is that you are not defined by what has happened in your past. You are defined by how you respond. See this in God's word to the prophet Joel.

> Fear not, O land; be glad and rejoice: for the LORD will do great things.
>
> Be not afraid, ye beasts of the field: for the pastures of the wilderness do spring, for the tree beareth her fruit, the fig tree and the vine do yield their strength.
>
> Be glad then, ye children of Zion, and rejoice in the LORD your God: for he hath given you the former rain moderately,

and he will cause to come down for you the rain, the former rain, and the latter rain in the first month.

And the floors shall be full of wheat, and the vats shall overflow with wine and oil.

And I will restore to you the years that the locust hath eaten, the cankerworm, and the caterpiller, and the palmerworm, my great army which I sent among you.

And ye shall eat in plenty, and be satisfied, and praise the name of the LORD your God, that hath dealt wondrously with you: and my people shall never be ashamed.

And ye shall know that I am in the midst of Israel, and that I am the LORD your God, and none else: and my people shall never be ashamed. (Joel 2:21-27)

These people endured incredible persecution and oppression. They had lost much; they had gone through incredible pain. Perhaps this is your story as well.

Stephaine and I recognized early on in our relationship that we had to deal with our losses if we were going to have a healthy relationship. For me, it was the loss of my first wife, Diane. Diane passed away after a battle with cancer at age 37 in 2005. We were married for eleven years, and I had to come to a place of wholeness before I could be all I needed to be for Stephaine. It was important for me to go through personal and group therapy in order to deal with my pain. I had to admit that for three years of my life after Diane's death I was so consumed with preserving her legacy that I had not given myself an opportunity to experience the joy of a new relationship. It was important for Stephaine to know me as Joseph first and not as Diane's husband. Likewise, it was important for me to see myself as Joseph first and not as Diane's husband.

Stephaine had lost her older sister, Wendy, a few years before we met and was still struggling with numerous questions herself.

Could she have done more? At the time of her sister's death, Stephaine was a resident physician. And while experiencing the pain of a sister dying unexpectedly at age 40, Stephaine had to be the voice of reason to her family in regard to what was transpiring before all their eyes. Wendy had been a mentor and "big sister," and Stephaine realized how important it was to deal with this pain so that she might be in a better position to move forward after dealing with her grief.

Our pain ended up being a point of connectivity in our relationship. We were able to communicate about it and be transparent about where we were in the process. I believe God brings people together who can identify with the depth of each other's pain. Our stories served as a catalyst for the development of our relationship. We cried together and gave each other permission to vent when necessary. Our relationship became a safe place, and consequently, over time, this created a level of trust between us. We were convinced that God had brought us together to remind us that He is a restorer. No matter how deep and acute the pain, a part of our destiny is working through that pain together.

You may be reading this book and wondering if things are going to turn out right in your situation. You're really wondering if what has happened in your life has already been the defining moment of your destiny. Is it too late? Is it too late for a new beginning? God's answer is "No."

GOD BROUGHT YOU TOGETHER

God has brought you together to work in His purpose, not apart from it. You are not competitors, rather companions. Healthy

3

> **To be a couple on a date with destiny means that you have to be in this together.**

couples have like vision and passions and are willing to make the necessary sacrifices for the success of the relationship. But, as an individual, if you don't know where you are going, it's hard to expect someone to go with you. **To be a couple on a date with destiny means that you have to be in this together. You have to be committed.**

Walking through our pain together means that we come out together on the other side. Stephaine and I have lived by this principle and it has blessed our relationship and marriage. You have to make a conscious decision to move forward and not become paralyzed by your pain. When God says in Isaiah 43:19 that "I will do a new thing: now it shall spring forth," He is saying He wants us to position ourselves spiritually, emotionally, and physically so that we can move forward, for it to happen.

I remember watching a young boy who was afraid to jump off the diving board into the deep water. He was comfortable with familiar surroundings; therefore, when he got on the diving board, he clung to it instead of jumping in, releasing himself into the water. I tell people all the time that you cannot "spring" if you "cling." You will never reach your full potential in relationships if you are holding on to things in your past. It's all right to have a history, but don't become a prisoner to your past. God has placed so much in you, and it *cannot* be eclipsed by your pain. We all come to a place where we have to decide if we are going to move ahead or stay stuck in the past. Will we wallow in the mire of our yesterday or will we pursue the greatness that lies ahead? Stephaine and I chose the latter, and I encourage you to do the same. We dealt with our past but then moved on. If we hadn't, we wouldn't be together today.

SHIFT TOWARD GREATNESS

God wants you to stop focusing so much on what has happened in the past. It's time for you as a child of God to make a shift. In other words, God is saying, "I'm moving you out of the season of your past pain, out of that season of destruction and despair. And I'm shifting you into a brand-new season where I'm getting ready to do some great and awesome things."

When God begins to shift you, things around you begin to happen. Sometimes you don't understand why they're happening, but God is literally moving you into the best days of your life. And even though you may have been wounded in your past, it's time to pick yourself up and declare, "What's ahead of me is better than what's been before!"

Something inside of you has to say, "This is my finest hour. So even with tears in my eyes, I have to convince myself that it's gonna get better up the road. Even if people laugh at me, even if you laugh at me, I know too much about God to know that God will not leave me in worse shape than He found me. He's going to take me to another

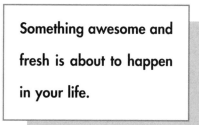

Something awesome and fresh is about to happen in your life.

dimension, another level." God wants you to know that your slate is clean; something awesome and fresh is about to happen in your life and in your life together as a couple.

DEVELOP A POSTURE OF ANTICIPATION

One thing we know for sure, God always makes good on His promises. Just like the prophet Joel says to a distressed people, he also says to us, "Fear not. Don't be afraid, but be glad and rejoice because the Lord will do great things. He's going to do great things for you" (adapted from Joel 2:21). Your part is to develop a posture of anticipation. Expect something. You can always tell when people are expecting something, because they receive revelation with anticipation.

I remember hearing a story about a group of folks who traveled down a dusty road each day to church in rural Louisiana. It was a community whose livelihood depended upon the crops coming in. They had been in a drought for several months, so the locals thought it would be a good thing to hold prayer services each night and pray for rain. Each night they passed down this road singing, enlisting others to join them in their pilgrimage to the prayer service at the church. And they were quite successful in enlisting willing participants; however, there was one man who refused to go along.

Mr. Brown would sit on his porch and shake his head, seemingly in agony as he watched them pass by day after day. They would ask him repeatedly to join them, but he refused time and time again. One day they all decided to go up and ask Mr. Brown why he wouldn't join their small town in their prayer meeting. It was their belief that everyone would benefit from the rain. They could not fathom why Mr. Brown was so stubborn. As they approached, a young man in his thirties with Bible in hand

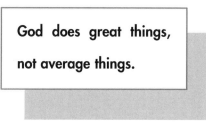

God does great things, not average things.

asked Mr. Brown on behalf of the group, "Why won't you attend our prayer services? We all need the rain, and if everybody joins in, we will have a better chance of the good Lord hearing us." Mr. Brown stood up from his old orange rocker, rickety and worn, and gazed at the small crowd in his yard. He fixed his eyes on the group and said with resounding conviction, "Because none of you have an umbrella. I watch each of you pass this way every evening going to pray for rain, but nobody ever takes an umbrella. I only pray where there is faith and expectation."

Expectation brings an umbrella. And if you are anticipating God doing something in your life, you have to bring your umbrella. When I pray for a thing, I believe that when I get off my knees it is already done. I've learned how to look like what I am asking God for. Stop looking at what you are going through and start looking like what you are going to.

Our God promises He's going to do great things for you, so live like what you expect to happen, will happen. **God does great things, not average things, not things like you and me, but great things.** Look around you. Stuff is happening. Even if it's not happening in your life, it's happening all around you. It's just a matter of time before the blessing comes into your life, because if God is blessing your neighbor, He's still in the neighborhood.

BEGIN TO THANK GOD FOR THE LITTLE STUFF

Once you understand that stuff **is** happening around you, light dawns. This understanding is a revelation that can shine the light on the areas of life that I take for granted, stuff I am overlooking. God says, "I'm tired of you people walking around with your lips stuck out, with your arms folded; you have an attitude, because I'm not doing what you think I ought to do." God says, "If you'll just look, I'm already doing some stuff, but because it isn't big enough for you, you think that the blessing is not going to come." Learn how to thank God for the little stuff first.

Thank God for the stuff He's doing right now, on the way to the blessing. You have an attitude, but you ought to thank God for the car you have; you ought to thank God for the house you have; you ought to thank God for the wife you have. God is for you, so who can be against you?

We spend too much time adding up our problems rather than counting our blessings. It's the little stuff that makes the difference on the way to destiny. I meet so many chronic complainers. These people are always alone. Nothing is ever good enough. They complain about everything. You will never be in a destiny-driven relationship if you are not appreciative. If you cannot appreciate the things that God does for you, then you will never be grateful for what your mate does.

I have learned in my relationship with Stephaine that the things that mean the most to her are the little things. I've seen her cry like a baby over little things that I thought were insignificant expressions of love, yet I've learned that they were more valuable than large, tangible things or my attempts at grand gestures.

My parents always told me to stay clear of people who didn't know how to say thank you. Ungrateful people never realize destiny because they go through life with entitlement issues. They feel that everyone owes them something. When you have entitlement issues, you are almost impossible to please. Expressions of kindness are often met with cynicism and criticism. Nobody wants to be in a relationship with this kind of person. It's not the kind of relationship that leads to destiny. It leads to your demise. Take a moment and reflect over the small things God has done in your life and give Him thanks for them. As you learn to do that, you will be more appreciative of the little things your mate does. It's the little things that count.

Think of some things you can do for your mate today. Do them without thought of getting a reward or something back. See what happens. If you don't get the results you want, don't give up. Keep trying.

Once you know stuff is happening, you'll start walking around with a spirit of readiness. Do you know how you can tell someone has that spirit? Just think of the people you know. They are the people who aren't concerned about what you think about them. And they are the people who say, "At any moment, God will do great things."

DELIVER US FROM EVIL

But sometimes we pray for deliverance. "Deliver me from my job." "Deliver me from my enemy." Sometimes we pray, "Lord, get me out of this." But God may say, "This is not the season. I'll keep you right in the mess, but I will give you a breakthrough right there so your enemy gets to see you blessed. I will prepare a table before you in the presence of your enemy."

I don't want to belittle your pain and suffering. Some of you may have been through deep, deep despair, perhaps at the hands of others, but also perhaps by your own hand. Some of you may be scarred by abuse, hatred, guilt, or violence; and you may be justified in feeling anger or hurt at the injustice of it all. I'm not advocating a quick fix and I'm not saying, "Don't worry, be happy." But I am saying that God knows your pain and can help you through it and then move you beyond it.

One of the most amazing stories in the Bible is the story of the three Hebrew boys in the fiery furnace. Their convictions put them there, yet they had faith to believe that God could deliver. Many of you reading this book have your own heated situations, and you are convinced that God can deliver. But if you examine how God delivered Shadrach, Meshach, and Abednego, it might give you some insight into how your deliverance will come. God did not deliver them **out** of the furnace; He delivered them **in** the furnace. They were free and unharmed, although the fire had been turned up to seven times its normal heat. They even came out without a scent of smoke.

God may not change your situation, but He will change you **in** it. So when you come through, you won't even smell like smoke. God uses moments like this to build character and faith. He will protect your destiny at all costs. Although you may experience temporary discomfort or even suffering, you must know that God is pushing you toward destiny.

YOUR TRUE DESTINY IS IN GOD'S HANDS

Once I begin to anticipate that God will do stuff in my life, I'm expecting God to show up, so I don't have to be afraid. I've dealt with the fear. This is true freedom, because it frees me to reach out to live, to love, to be fruitful and accept the blessings God has for me. The knots that have tied me up and bound my spirit are gone, allowing me to run the good race with my eyes on the prize.

Growing up is a process; maturity is a process; faith is a process; growing in love and Christian marriage is a process. God is a **process** God, especially when it comes to getting the blessing into lives. Blessings come as a process because of what the enemy does. The enemy systematically, categorically comes into your life. He calculates this thing, comes in, and assaults the people of God. The enemy doesn't just come in one time. He sits back, strategizes how he's going to take your family out, how he's going to come at your mind, come at your money, come at your marriage; that's how the enemy does. Sometimes the enemy will wait years before he launches his assault. And God might allow these things to happen. But God also says that there is a process and that your destiny is never defined by what happened in the past. Your destiny, your future, is in God's hands.

IT WAS WORTH IT

We all know that the road is not easy. Our question is, "Is it worth it?"

And it shall come to pass afterward, that I will pour out my spirit upon all flesh; and your sons and your daughters shall prophesy, your old men shall dream dreams, your young men shall see visions: And also upon the servants and upon the handmaids in those days will I pour out my spirit. And I will shew wonders in the heavens and in the earth, blood, and fire, and pillars of smoke. The sun shall be turned into darkness, and the moon into blood, before the great and the terrible day of the LORD come. And it shall come to pass, that whosoever shall call on the name of the LORD shall be delivered: for in mount Zion and in Jerusalem shall be deliverance, as the LORD hath said, and in the remnant whom the LORD shall call. (Joel 2:28-32)

God never promised that just because He reveals our destiny to us, our end result to us, that the devil is not going to do everything to discourage us from arriving at the place where God intends us to be. We can see this plain truth in what the prophet Joel says to the people of God. Everything that has happened in your life was really worth it. Whether good or bad, when you look back over your life, when you reflect on what God gives you as a result of persevering, then you can look back and thank God for what He's allowed to happen. Because what I've gone through has developed character; it has developed patience; it has developed dependency on God like never before. And this allows God to release something in your life regarding your destiny—the next dimension of blessings. This is not to say that it may not take some time to come to this realization. But God and Christian friends can help.

I know personally that the right people in your life are a great blessing during the most difficult times of your life. God blessed me with friends who told me the truth. The Bible says in Proverbs 27:6 that "faithful are the wounds of a friend; but the kisses of an enemy are deceitful." It's important that you pray for strategic friendships. We all need people in our lives who can speak to our destiny. I was fortunate to have friends who would never let me slip into despair. They would remind me of God's promise over my life. They would hold me accountable and keep me focused on what God was doing

What you've gone through has qualified you.

in my life. The amazing thing about God is that He will always connect you with like-minded people who see your "not yet."

YOU'VE BEEN QUALIFIED

You have been knocked down and may be, even now, down for the count. You may need some help getting back up. You may be battered and bruised, but what you've gone through has qualified you. There is the hope. God will not allow His spirit into people who have not proven their integrity in tough times. He will not trust His Spirit to people who will not acknowledge that it was His power that got them where they are.

I remember speaking with a friend named James. James was having difficulty reconciling why he was experiencing so many bad things at the same time. He had recently lost his job, experienced the death of his mother as well as a cousin, and had gone through a nasty breakup with his girlfriend. As you can imagine, James was disillusioned and discouraged. Our talks often involved him reminding me how life had dealt him a bad hand and how God was punishing him for things he had done in his past. I had to remind James that God was preparing him for his destiny.

These things have not come to destroy you; they have come to develop you. You will never know what you can handle until you are put in a situation to confront it. I reminded James of something I want to remind you of as well. Every story leads to a greater glory. God uses the substance of our story to propel us to new levels of glory. Don't allow what you are experiencing to make you turn away from God. He is strategically using these events to mature you and prepare you for where He is taking you. If God allowed it, it has to bless you. Today James thanks God for what he was bitter about a year ago. Perhaps that's why the James of the Bible declared that we should "count it all joy when [we] fall into divers temptations" (James 1:2).

Every tear, every hater, every person who quit on me, every person who walked out on me, every person who lied to me—all of it was worth it, because all things work together for good for those who love God and are called according to His purpose. What the devil didn't realize when he threw all that stuff at me to destroy my life was that God would use it to develop me.

AVAILABILITY IS BETTER THAN ABILITY

After you have proven yourself credible and that God can trust you with trouble, that's when He will pour out His Spirit. And when He does, He says, "I'm going to pour it out among **all** flesh, men and women, young and old." To really appreciate this, you have to understand that in biblical days women were considered unimportant. They were considered property—in many cases they had no more rights than animals. And here God speaks back into that culture and says, "I'm getting ready to do something that goes against culture. I'm getting ready to use people, who people think cannot be used. I'm moving beyond gender, I'm moving beyond age. I'm moving beyond color. It doesn't matter what side of the track you were born on." God says, "When I pour out my spirit, I'm not pouring it out to people who have the **ability**, I'm pouring it out to people who have the **availability**."

It is incredibly important that you put yourself in position for God to use you. Stop reminding God of your deficiencies and shortcomings. He already knows. The only reason God uses imperfect people is because He has nobody else to choose from. Imagine the power of purpose in a relationship rooted in availability.

⤷ One of the biggest challenges among couples is availing themselves to each other. With our hectic schedules, many couples live by their calendars. They literally have to make appointments to spend quality time with each other. The excuses and the clutter that crowd our lives breed contempt in our relationships. If people cannot make themselves available for God to use their gifts and talents, then it is highly probable that they will not make themselves available to each other. God wants to use us to bring His will to pass on earth. There are a lot of people who **can** do, but **will not** do. This strains our relationships with God and with others.

Everyday I wake up, I ask God to use me wherever and however He needs to. I'm available to Him. Availability has become a lifestyle that

> **God honors your availability over your ability.**

15

> **God speaks not to your reality, but to your possibility.**

has also permeated our marriage. Stephaine and I both are tremendously busy. My ministry schedule and her medical schedule are brutal; yet we avail ourselves to God's purpose because our destiny is greater than our personal desires.

GOD SPEAKS TO YOUR POSSIBILITY

God does not only speak to your "right now." He also speaks to your "not yet." You've got enough people speaking to your right now; you already know how bad it is right now. God says, "I don't want you to develop a 'blues theology' that reaffirms to you why you're crying and gives you all kinds of permission to whine and have a pity-party, and sit back and sing the blues about how bad things are."

The moment we begin to receive our gift from God, our perspective changes. We dream dreams; we see visions. We make ourselves available for what God wants to do in our lives, in our marriage, in our family, with our friends. God responds by widening our perspective.

It is an amazing thing when two visions become one. Whatever God is showing you, He has placed similar destiny in the person He has ordained for your life. Remember, destiny is how a thing ends up. Vision is a glimpse of the end result of purpose. As you walk in relationship with someone, you should discover similar values and ideals.

Although Stephaine and I are in different fields, we share a vision of making our communities better. She is committed to making our community better through health and awareness, and I am committed to the same vision through spirituality and empowerment. Though the methodologies are different, the goal is the same. I often tell my staff that the effectiveness of vision is when we focus not on the "role" but on the "goal." It doesn't matter who gets the credit as long as the objective is met. Whatever God does through you as a couple, remember it is larger than your independent agendas.

This vision can also live beyond you. We dream knowing that the generation behind us will realize what we can only dream of now. Martin Luther King, Jr., had a dream that he knew would not be fulfilled in his lifetime, but we have seen that dream come to pass in ours. So when God says that He is going to deposit vision in you, once He gives you a "not yet" word, then God says, "What I'm going to do is, I'm going to start **showing** you what I just **spoke** to you."

When God called me to preach, I was twenty years old at Southern University. I was already going to law school, had everything straight; I was on my way. It's good to go to law school, but God called me to preach, and God sent me to Nashville, Tennessee, to Vanderbilt Divinity School. Understand this, I'm twenty-one years old now, I'm coming to Nashville, Tennessee— I have never heard of Nashville, Tennessee, other than *Hee Haw*. I didn't know what was in Nashville; I just knew God called me. But I went, and two years later, God put the vision inside of me.

God told me, "Now, son, this vision I could not give you when I first called you, because you had not gone through enough to be a good steward of it. That's why I don't call people on Sunday and let them pastor on Tuesday, because they hadn't been through enough." He says now, "But understand that this vision is very important." So I know this is different, because it's like I had a Damascus Road experience. It was like my eyes were blinded and when I opened them up I saw the world totally differently. We would be driving down the street and people would see dilapidated buildings, and I'd see condominiums. People would see cow pastures and I would see strip malls; people would see grocery stores and an old nightclub and I'd see an Antioch church location. Here's the deal—after a while when nobody was seeing what I was seeing, I started thinking I was crazy. But I kept on seeing it, and soon others saw it too.

GOD'S CHOICE IS GOD'S INVOICE

The vision that God gives you is essential and He promises that if you keep this **vision** under **divine supervision**, He will always give you **provision**, and you will never have **division** or a need for **revision**. So I have never had a vision that I could afford, because if you have a vision that you can afford, it's not a vision. It's just a good idea. Vision is always bigger than your budget. It's always bigger than the money you have.

> **If you keep this vision under divine supervision, He will always give you provision, and you will never have division or a need for revision.**

Does that make you upset? Good, because if it's God's will, it's God's bill.

If it's God's choice; it's God's invoice. You don't have to worry about how you're going to pay for what God showed you! Mt. Zion Church is a 17-million-dollar facility that we began building with only $30,000 in the bank. You never have to have the money when God gives you a vision, because if you keep the vision where God wants it to be, you'll always have provision. But this does not mean that God wants you to have a new car every time you drive past the dealer's showroom. Letting God pick up the tab is not an excuse for being irresponsible.

When your perspective changes, God will send the vision, and that vision, God's vision, will always outlive the visionary. I started pastoring Mt. Zion when I was 24 years old. Do you really think that when I'm in my 70s, I'm going to be running between services? No, I'm going to be on my yacht in the Atlantic watching some young guy up here do his thing. Why? Because I recognize that if the vision of Mt. Zion dies when I retire, it wasn't under God's supervision. Mt. Zion's purpose is to get better when I retire. Mt. Zion's best days are to yet to come, because a good man leaves an inheritance to his children's children; a good couple plans together for the benefit of their children and grandchildren.

If your stuff dies with you, then something's wrong with it from the jump. The vision has to outlive you. Your vision for your family, your vision for your spouse, your vision for your neighborhood—if your vision is from God and remains under His supervision, it's going to live on. It's your children's inheritance.

GOD MEETS ME IN MY MESS

"Yes," you say, "but my life is still in a mess." But like Jesus asked the "certain man" He met by the pool of Besthesda in John, chapter 5, Jesus says to you, "Do you want to be made whole? Get up, take up your bed and walk." And the man was made whole and took up his bed and walked. God met him in his mess, and He will deliver you too.

GOD DOES NOT DELIVER YOU FROM NOTHING

God does not deliver from nothing; He delivers from something, even if it is your own mess. So it is that something that I thank Him for. 'Cause if I hadn't gotten into something, I wouldn't have known He could get me out of it. Please realize that the devil is trying to get you to give up on school; he's trying to get you to give up on your family, on your vision, on your destiny. Do you want to know why? Because he knows that he can't take from you what God promises. But the devil is a liar! And he has messed with the wrong somebody. Because when God delivers us, God knows we have big mouths and God knows we are going to tell somebody what He did for us. God will meet you where you are.

Oftentimes we allow ourselves to become discouraged because of the situation we are in. God's word to you today is that He cares. No matter what mistakes or messes you've made, your destiny is salvageable. I meet so many people who have come out of unhealthy relationships and feel like it's all over. They wonder if they can go on. They speculate whether or not what they desire is even possible. God's word to you today is that you are never so low that the grace of God can't find you. Your life may be a mess now, but God can turn it into a miracle. I've made a mess of my life on numerous occasions. I've gotten ahead of God. I've listened to bad advice from friends. I've moved on my raw emotions without praying and ended up in places inconsistent with my destiny. The good news is that I'm writing this book as evidence that it's not over until God says so.

You don't have to have it all together. You might be messed up, tore up from the floor up, but the good news is that God looks beyond your faults and supplies your needs. Yeah, we are all messed up; we haven't always been where we are. The Lord will meet you right in your mess, right where you are lying all bent and crippled. He will reach out and ask you if you want to be whole.

When we're introduced to this "certain man," the Bible wants us to know that we are like this man. He is a certain person who has been in his particular situation for thirty-eight years—a long time. And every time his breakthrough was going to come, the moment he got ready to get in the pool, somebody pushed him out of the way and jumped in before him. Somebody got his promotion, took his credit, stole his thunder. But then something powerful happens, because Jesus comes by and sees him as more than his suffering, knows that he has no one to help him, and, in a word, Jesus changes everything. Jesus not only cures his infirmity but heals him from the inside out. Jesus cures the disease but also connects him to his ultimate purpose and destiny in God.

You may believe that you're *going to have* a date with destiny someday, but you're also wondering just how long you have to

| God's about to show up in your life. |

wait for God to start blessing you. You might even be frustrated by the process of waiting on things to happen. Your patience might be about gone. But you've got a date, you're in God's PDA, and God's about to show up in your life. He's about to do something you've been expecting Him to do; He's about to break some rules on your behalf; He's about to do something unorthodox in order to get your miracle in your life. God is about to meet you in your mess. It doesn't matter how long you've been there, doesn't matter how low you've been, doesn't matter what people have labeled you, how they look at you, what they call you. The truth is that God's about to turn your situation around and connect you to your purpose.

FINDING YOUR GREATNESS AS A COUPLE

1. As a couple, talk about what first attracted you to each other.
2. Make a list of the blessings God has already given you.
3. Share with each other how God has qualified you.
4. Talk about how you can make yourselves more available to God.
5. What makes you a great couple?
6. Make a date with each other and celebrate your future together.
7. If you don't already, start praying together.

CHAPTER TWO

CHASING DESTINY: GOD'S HAND IS UPON YOU

God will shift you and help you develop a posture of anticipation. You must learn to thank Him for stuff no matter how small. He lets you know that it's all worth it and He holds your destiny in His hands. With God in your life, you realize that you're called to be available and that you're qualified, that all things are possible and work together for the good. Your life may be a mess right now, but as a couple, start walking together, holding hands, going on the greatest date possible—your date with destiny.

MOLD ME, MAKE US

The word which came to Jeremiah from the LORD, saying,

Arise, and go down to the potter's house, and there I will cause thee to hear my words.

Then I went down to the potter's house, and, behold, he wrought a work on the wheels.

> And the vessel that he made of clay was marred in the hand
> of the potter: so he made it again another vessel, as seemed
> good to the potter to make it.
> Then the word of the LORD came to me, saying,
> O house of Israel, cannot I do with you as this potter? saith
> the LORD. Behold, as the clay is in the potter's hand, so are ye
> in mine hand, O house of Israel. (Jeremiah 18:1-6)

One of the greatest revelations that any of us could come to in life is that we are constantly evolving. That is, our relationship with God is progressive. And regardless of where we think people should be, we have to understand that they are in process. And we are in process. God is working through our lives, crafting us, molding us to be the people that ultimately we are to become. The good news is that God knows what my end ought to be. And therefore God is more patient with me than most people are. A lot of people give up on us because they don't realize what God's intent is for our lives. The truth is, and what we must understand is, what Jeremiah came to understand—we are nothing but clay in the hands of the Potter. And He has a will and a purpose for your life.

That is why God allows certain things to happen to you and not to other people. God is molding you as a person, as a couple, as a family, as a community of believers. We are in the middle of an incredible process of development, and God is shaping us by every experience so that the greatness inside of us can come into fruition.

You can't know your value until you've come through the experiences that God has allowed you to go through. And that's why I've just made up my

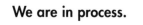

We are in process.

mind: Lord, whatever I have to go through, mold me, make me; it's all right with me. Whoever I've got to let go of, whatever I've got to leave behind, I'm ready. I'll do what you want me to do. I'll go where you want me to go. All things work together for God's glory, and in the end, everything will be all right.

GOD WILL REPOSITION YOU

Perhaps you've gone through enough stuff. Get ready, because God has you right where He wants you. He calls you to be greater. There are two things about a call from God. The first is that God always repositions you when He calls you. He always moves you from the place of comfort to a place of challenge and conviction. You can never stay in the place where you are. You may want to be in a place of convenience and a place of com-placency, a place where you are comfortable. But when there is a mandate on your life to do greater things, you have to get out of your comfort zone.

When God called Abraham, He told him to leave his country, leave with his wife and go to a place that God would show him. When God called Jonah, Jonah didn't want to go, because he didn't like those people and he didn't really care if they were on the way to destruction. But he was called—it didn't matter that he tried to run away. When God gets ready for you, he'll move heaven and earth to get to you. His ever-seeking love will find you wherever you are. He might even move you out of the

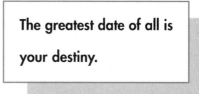

The greatest date of all is your destiny.

25

boat of your own father, like He did His disciples, Peter, James, and John, to take you on the grandest fishing trip possible, the trip of your ultimate destiny.

GOD REVEALS YOUR DESTINY

God repositions you, but then in that call He gives you revelation. Perhaps He's called you before. Perhaps you haven't really heard God, but God can cause you to hear His words and can speak to you as never before. God will speak to your destiny but He needs you to be committed.

The only way your destiny is going to become visible is for you to put yourself into God's hands. Like clay, we can be lumpy and inconsistent, but we are also works in process. You know about playdough. You take your little lump of playdough, build your little house, but all it takes is somebody coming in and messing with it and it falls apart. Build your little man with playdough and all it takes is some little stray wind to come through and blow your man's arm off, blow your man's head off. All you do is pick up the pieces and try to mesh it together again. We're like clay, God says, but not completely. We are much more valuable and God doesn't play around with us. He loves us and is careful with us. He's not out to stick it to us, and He doesn't take pleasure in the bad things that happen to us.

STAY IN THE PRESSURE

In my meditation time, God let me see this for myself. I sat down and in my imagination saw the potter working on the wheel. I said, "God show me what you showed Jeremiah." I saw the potter with his foot moving the pedal to make the wheel move, and I saw the clay spinning. It started out as a lump, but every time the potter patted his foot, the clay went to spinning. I said, "God, what are you trying to show me?" He said, "Tell My people that's what I do to their lives. They start out as nothing but a lump, but I got to take them through circumstances, like the time someone lied to you, the time somebody walked out, the time they lost a job, the time somebody broke **your** heart."

But then it got more personal. I said, "Wait a minute, God, You know I'm Your man now. And sometimes I feel like Job. God, the devil's messing with my mind. Three years ago, I lost my wife. Sometimes the church wondered if I'd show up to preach Your word." But God said, "Go back and tell them this, tell them that while the clay is spinning, I still got My hand on it. Tell them the only way the clay can become what I want it to become is, I have to apply some pressure. And if the clay will stay in the pressure, stay in the pressure, stay in the pressure . . ."

God is molding you. Cry if you have to cry. There may be pain for the night, but joy is coming in the morning. I know you have suffered. Maybe it's been abuse at the hands of your father, maybe it's been violence at the hands of a gang member, maybe you've been beaten, stomped on, victimized, lost those you love, those you'd

> **Stay in the pressure; call on God's name; get into the Word; talk to your pastor; but most of all, don't give up.**

have given your own life for. But stay in the pressure, call on God's name, get into the Word, talk to your pastor, but most of all, don't give up. God has His hand on you. You may be dizzy from all the spinning, but God is doing a great thing in you. He is moving your destiny from actuality to potentiality.

FROM ACTUALITY TO POTENTIALITY

One of the most important decisions that any of us can make is to choose how we look at our reality. Understanding the following two perspectives can contribute to how your destiny will unfold. The first is actuality. Actuality looks at circumstance and says, "Accept things as they are; this is the way it's going to unfold for you. Nothing is going to change." As a result, whenever you walk in actuality, you have limited vision that can't stretch beyond your right now.

For instance there are people who embark upon relationships at face value. The true potential lies within the work necessary to evolve together into what God intends. Yes, there should be certain standards up front; however, if you approach it from actuality, you limit what is possible. Each of you will change. Each of you can grow and move toward destiny. So many couples get discouraged because they stop at actuality. They allow the challenges and frustrations of right now to skew the potential of their relationship.

When Stephaine and I first met, we had already accomplished much; yet we both knew that there was so much more to accomplish. Healthy relationships never arrive; they are always evolving, they are always on their way to something greater. When you see yourself as "becoming," then you will appreciate the evolution taking place within your mate. The fact that your mate is changing should not surprise or even alarm you. You're changing too. The issue is whether or not that change is in God's direction.

The second way to look at circumstances is potentiality. Potentiality looks at what is possible. It moves beyond what is actual and embraces what is possible in your reality. Potentiality is that thing that stretches you beyond the facts and allows you to transcend to faith. It is that thing that says, "Regardless of what is right now, this is not the way the story will end." Potentiality says that there is something that God is yet able to do in spite of what my situation looks like. Actuality keeps you focused on your "right now," but potentiality lifts your eyes to your "not yet."

To give you an idea of the difference between living in actuality and potentiality, look at the story of Jabez in the Bible. The story is found in 1 Chronicles, chapter 4. While the Bible doesn't really say a lot about Jabez, we are told that he is an honorable man. And we are told that he was born out of his mother's great sorrow.

I had a colorful childhood growing up. My mother would probably attest that when I was born I caused her great pain. Medically I struggled, and socially I was the difficult child. I didn't do too well in school, and a lot of folks wrote me off early on. What I refused to do was allow my childhood to dictate my destiny. There are many people who go through life satisfied to be victims of a dysfunctional childhood. Rather than taking this route, we should realize the potential resident within us.

When the Bible says that Jabez was an honorable man, it means that he was a man of character. When God gets ready to bless somebody, he's looking for somebody he can trust with a blessing—someone with character.

GOD CAN ENLARGE YOUR CAPACITY

This man of character was also a man of prayer. And in prayer Jabez asks God, "Lord, bless me indeed, enlarge my coasts; give me more capacity to receive." Jabez is not asking for a thing; he is asking for God to accommodate the thing. (That thing can be a vision or the dream in you.) After surveying his surroundings, Jabez realized that if the thing in him were to manifest in his present context, it would not fit. Maybe there is something that God has deposited in you that God can't bring out of you yet, because you're around small-thinking people. These folk can't appreciate what God wants to do in your life.

One of the things that I tell people in pursuit of healthy relationships is never apologize for your standards. Your standards are a safeguard from foolishness. When you understand your value, then other people will appreciate it. The old adage is true that "birds of a feather flock together." You will attract what you are and intimidate what you don't need.

Think about all the time you wasted trying to elevate people to your level but they never arrived. This is not a statement of arrogance, rather it is a declaration of confidence. Some people are only designed to go to certain levels with you. The space shuttle takes off at an amazing speed to reach orbit. It is assisted by rocket boosters. An amazing thing happens when it reaches a certain altitude. The rocket boosters fall off. Now, there is nothing wrong with the rocket boosters or the shuttle. The rocket boosters are functioning properly, because they are not designed to hang on after a certain altitude. If they don't fall off, they will prevent the shuttle from reaching its orbit. There are a lot of people who we meet who are like rocket boosters, and we try to make them a permanent fixture as we pursue destiny. What God will do in order to assure that you reach your destiny is create a situation where they will fall off. It's not a bad thing, because they were never meant to fly in your orbit. Stop whining over who fell off and start expecting people in your life who can handle where God is about to take you.

I don't know about you, but I'm tired of having to downsize my potential just so I can fit in certain cliques, just so certain people will like me, just so I will impress certain people. I'm so tired of coming down to some folk's level. I've just made up my mind. I want to be around people who are going to upgrade me. I want to be in relationships that upgrade me, and I want to help upgrade others.

"And God granted him that which he requested." Now, when your reality reaches to potentiality, you're able to see how God says, "I can trust people who reach beyond the now." Okay, if the events of your life are defined by the now, your sight is limited only to what God does now. Consequently, if God doesn't do what you think He ought to do now, then you get mad at God, but God's not responding to your now. See, God may be telling you "No" now, so that it may not happen until five years from now. When you look back over your life, you'll thank God for the mountains, and the storms, and the battles He brought you through. If I never had a problem, I wouldn't know what faith in God's Word could do.

So potentiality is about faith. Faith is the substance of things hoped for, the evidence of things not seen. Faith is about potentiality if you can believe that all things are possible to those who

> **Set yourself up for favor.**

believe. So when you walk in righteousness and you walk in faith, then you set yourself up for favor.

When you look at Jabez's life, he was asking for something that was socially, politically, domestically unachievable. He asked for something that his society said he wasn't supposed to have. But God gave him the desires of his heart. Perhaps the reason you're reading this book is to change your situation. Perhaps you need to know that what you've been through, you've not been through in vain. Perhaps everybody's labeled you or given up on you. God's about to fill the stadium with all your haters, bring you to the fifty yard line and shine the spotlight and say, "Look at what I can do to somebody who dared to move beyond reality and reach beyond what people said was possible. Look who I chose."

KNOW THAT YOU'RE CHOSEN

First Timothy 2:9 says that we are a chosen generation; we are a royal priesthood. And as Matthew says in 22:14, "Many are called, but few are chosen." When you are chosen, it means that you have been made the recipient of the sovereign grace of God. God is the king; He is sovereign. He can do whatever He wants, and when He extends grace to you, you begin to let people know that "I got it." It was not because I asked for it; I didn't choose this, but it chose me. Some people hate you because maybe you got the position and they didn't, maybe you got into the program and they didn't. Just tell them, "I'm sorry; I'm just chosen. Take it up with God, because God has a way of looking out for folk—out for you."

GOD'S INVESTED IN YOU

So does that mean I don't suffer? You might ask, why am I going through the stuff I'm going through? You may want everybody to think that you've got it together, but you may have stuff that you can't even talk about to anybody. But don't despair, God's got too much invested in you to let the enemy take you out. You've got to understand that the devil isn't after you, he's after what God is trying to do through you. That's why you don't take the attack personally, that's why you don't let yourself get depressed—because you understand how to handle the blessing. When you are chosen, you've got to say, "Lord, give me the courage to handle being chosen, because if I don't suffer with You, I cannot reign with You."

YOU ARE FINER THAN GOLD

How do you go through it? You must see what God allows you to go through as a part of His will. My friend Pastor Marvin Sapp says, "He saw the best in me." If you could ever see yourself like God sees you and not like people who have hurt you see you, you will begin to appreciate the process. One of the things we've all discovered during the financial crisis, called the recession, is that gold held its value. In many instances it increased in value. Regardless of what happened to the economy, the stabilizer was gold. When relationships are able to endure transitions and challenges, it's because the individuals within them have been tried like gold. God allowed you to go through it not just for you, but for the sake of the relationship He has destined for your life.

> **Your faith is more precious than gold.**

First Peter 1:6 says, "Ye greatly rejoice, though now for a season, if need be, ye are in heaviness through manifold temptations." That means many different kinds of temptations, trials, tests, storms; but he says now, "The trial of your faith [is] much more precious than . . . gold that perisheth, though it be tried with fire." When you are chosen, you look at yourself like you are gold, and you have to recognize that you're going to go through trials like gold goes through the fire.

Two things happen to gold when it goes through the fire. One is that everything that is attached to gold that brings gold's value down burns away. Right now, you may be going through some things and you've been saying, "My God, how do I get this person out of my life? They won't let me go." God answers and says, "I'll keep you in something long enough that you won't have to ask them to let you go, they'll volunteer for it." Some folks just feed off your life. And you can give God glory when they're gone, because they were bringing your value down.

The second thing fire does to gold is that the longer gold stays in the fire, the greater its value. The more fire you go through, the greater character you can have. You may not fully understand your value, but God does. And He knows the effect of all the trials and tribulations you've been through. He knows the lessons you've learned, the people you've reached out to—your gains and your pains. He knows if these fiery trials have made you more real or more fake.

Do you know how to tell the difference between real gold and fake gold? They look the same and even shine the same. The difference comes with the rain and storm. Baby, the fake stuff is going to change, it's going to tarnish, but the real stuff is going to stand. The longer you stand in the fire, the more you are refined and the more God can use you for His glory.

GOD CHOSE US TO BE TOGETHER

I had the opportunity to speak with a young lady in my congregation who is intelligent, beautiful, and independent. She expressed to me her frustrations in connecting with a certain gentleman in my church who by all accounts is an amazingly successful brother. After a few years of the emotional "roller coaster" of indecision in their relationship, she began to wonder if it was worthwhile to continue investing in someone who did not reciprocate. She was clearly more involved than he was. Though he is a great guy, they were on different pages. What I have discovered is two great people do not automatically make a great relationship. I advised her to think about herself more and not remain with a man who did not fully appreciate who she was.

We miss our date with destiny because we are emotionally tied to people who don't appreciate the totality of who we really are. I pleaded with her to let it go and chase destiny. Never put your dreams and goals on hold. When you chase destiny, whoever really connects with you will affirm the greatness that's in you.

CHASING DESTINY

It's important to live your life chasing what God intends for you. And whatever happens, the good, the bad, the ugly, the ups, the downs, the setbacks, the layoffs, whatever happens, it is all designed to push you to the place of destiny. This is really about your will and what you will do. Will you live your life continuously allowing your past to hinder you from the promise that God has for your future? Will you continue to be paralyzed by bad situations in your past and allow the frustrations of yesterday to hinder you from the things that God has for your tomorrow? Will you allow yourself to be running after people who don't value you, who don't appreciate you, who don't really embrace the value and gifts in your life? Or will you embrace destiny?

One of the things I have discovered is that God knows what we need better than we do. I have seen people with such unrealistic expectations that you could truly believe that only Jesus would qualify to be with them. Though comical, it is true. It is important to know that God connects us providentially to the person He chooses. Yes, He allows us to be agents of free will; yet, if we follow His lead, He will direct us where we need to be. Proverbs 3:5-6 says, "Lean not unto thine own understanding. In all thy ways acknowledge him, and he shall direct thy paths."

When God brings two people together, He is thinking about the product of that relationship. Before your grandfather met your grandmother, God was thinking about you. You are the offspring of the providential work of God. At this present moment God is preparing someone to be with you. That person is going through a series of events to develop into the person you need in your life. The same is happening with you. Although the encounter may not have happened, once you meet, you will share similar stories as confirmation of God's providence at work.

The likelihood of a busy pastor connecting with a neonatologist from Harvard was slim to none. Considering our lifestyles and circles, we could not have come together of our own accord. God chose us to be together. Long before we knew it, He brought us full circle. I didn't know Stephanie was a member of my church during the first two years of my pastorate. We never met prior to her going off to medical school. I know now it was God's will. As the years passed, God allowed both of us to experience life in ways that matured us and molded us into the people we are today. Had we met prior to God's timing, we might not be together now. Remember well that God knows the exact time to make this connection.

Don't panic. Don't get ahead of God. Many people try to find their spouse with the mouse on the computer. Although I can appreciate your putting yourself in position to be "found," it is essential that you maintain patience in order for God to connect you. My wife Stephaine's mom would always tell her, "What you are looking for is looking for you." She's right, you may be thousands of miles away, but if God chooses it, He will order your steps at the right season to discover it.

Will you declare and make up your mind: "I'm after destiny. I'm not after some position; I'm not chasing some person; I'm not chasing nothing, no platform—I just want destiny"? When you're after destiny, you get to a point in your life that you recognize that even if a person closes a door on me, it doesn't matter, because God will open up doors for people who are after destiny. When you're after destiny, you don't have to kiss anybody's behind to get what God has for your life. God's got blessings for people who want destiny.

THE POWER OF FOCUS

That's why you've got to understand the power of focus. Because Paul says in Philippians 3:13 that "This one thing I do."

He has to focus on one thing. You've got to understand that focus is really about moving away from deadly distractions and fatal distractions, because you don't allow people to define for you what your assignment is. There are too many people who live vicariously through the dreams and ideas of other people. But you need to understand what focus is all about. There is something that God placed in your spirit, there is something that keeps you up at night. That's the thing where you're on your job and you're frustrated and you say, "I know there is something else I ought to be doing. There is something that I keep carrying in my belly but that nobody else will understand." That's the thing you ought to be chasing. Not what somebody said you look like you ought to be, or what you ought to do because you're into making everybody else happy, because you'll be miserable. No, I've made up my mind, my days of being miserable are over. My days of trying to make everybody else happy are over; I've got to do what God called me to do. That's why I'm not trying to fit in with your little crowd; I don't have to be in your clique; I ain't got time to sit around with silly people who aren't going anywhere. I'm chasing destiny! I got stuff to do. I'm focused.

LIVING WITH THAT BIG ERASER

But then Paul says, "Brethren, I count not myself to have apprehended," he says, "but this one thing I do, forgetting those things which are behind, and reaching forth unto those things which are before." I put my past in perspective. You know, one of the things that hinders so many of us is our inability to deal with our past issues. All of us in this place have some past failures. Doesn't matter how anointed you are, doesn't matter how many tongues you speak in, how big your Bible is, all of us have some things in our past we're not proud of. All of us wish we had a big ol' eraser.

All of us have some stuff in our past we wish we could forget, times we missed the mark, people we didn't do right, relationships and friendships we know didn't bring glory to God. And if you're going to chase destiny, you got to remember now that your failures didn't have to be fatal. You can pick yourself up, brush yourself off, and start afresh.

Just like the young lady I advised to go forward, many of you need to brush yourself off and go forward. I remember when I was in the eleventh grade and could not get a date to the prom or a girl to go out with me at all. I was crushed over the ordeal; however, I remember my mother telling me that I was an awesome young man and one day some woman was going to appreciate me. I never forgot those words. I want you to know what my mother told me, "You are awesome. One day someone will appreciate and value you." Don't you slip into depression and linger in discouragement. Your best season is ahead of you.

So you got to understand something: the amazing thing about God is that God forgives you of stuff people won't forget. They're still talking about your past and you're in a whole other chapter of your life. You have moved on and shifted, and they're still talking about your old stuff. Don't let them know where you are; they are stuck in yesterday. See, but that's why you have

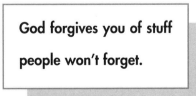

God forgives you of stuff people won't forget.

to make up your mind that this is not about your past, it's about your future. I refuse to be a victim. I'm done; I'm done; I'm through rehearsing what happened to me.

I'm through giving the devil the victory; every time somebody calls, talking about, "What they did to me, what happened to me, what I've been through." There comes a time you gotta say, "Wait a minute now, I cannot keep rehearsing this in my spirit. God has put it behind. Yup, it happened, I acknowledge it, maybe I've been to counseling, but the Lord has brought me a mighty long way." See, you don't give yourself enough credit. Some of you have endured some stuff that has destroyed other people and while you're sitting up talking about how bad it was, you ought to just give God glory that you survived it. You ought to thank God that even though you were troubled on every side you were not perplexed. You were cast down, but you were not destroyed. You learned how to count it all joy when you fell into dire temptation. You decided that weeping may endure for a night, but joy comes in the morning. You're a survivor.

LOOK THROUGH YOUR WINDSHIELD, NOT YOUR REARVIEW MIRROR

Then, this one thing I do: forget those things which are behind. I cannot keep bringing up the stuff in my past. See, there is a reason why your rearview mirror is smaller than your windshield. One is for staring, and one is for glancing. And if you find yourself staring in the wrong one, there's nothing wrong with just saying, "Oh, OK, but I'm still keeping my eye on my windshield!" Many of the wrecks you've had in your life happened because you stared too long in the rearview mirror.

DESTINY KEEPS ME IN POSITION TO GET THE PRIZE

Paul says, "I press toward the mark for the prize of the high calling of God in Christ Jesus." Now, what you've got to do is press toward the mark. This is why purpose is so important, because destiny keeps me in position to get the prize. It keeps me focused on my windshield. Paul admits something. Many of us have discovered that going toward destiny is not easy. Anybody chasing destiny will tell you that with that chase comes stress and strain. You're gonna need internal fortitude, you're gonna need the resolve to overcome the many obstacles the devil throws in your life to derail your destiny.

This is how you know you're really close to your destiny. It's like the devil sits in his office and tells all his demons, "Cancel everybody on my schedule but them." It's like he ain't got nobody else to mess with but you. Anybody ever felt like that? Like, "Isn't there somebody else you can mess with besides me?" That's when I know I'm close. Because you are more of a threat to Satan's kingdom when you get closer to destiny.

Whenever a relationship is headed toward destiny, it is subject to the most persecution it has ever seen. How many times have you asked, "Are we under attack?" Satan knows what God's intentions are regarding your relationship with this person. He's not going to sit idly by and watch you glide with God's purpose in mind and simply receive God's blessings. So you've got to be smart and be on your game and know your spot, your position, and your route.

In football they have a play called a timing pattern. The wide receiver runs down the field ten yards then seven yards across, then waits for the quarterback to throw the ball. The defensive back hits him at the line of scrimmage to discourage and prevent him from running his route; at the very least the defensive back wants to mess up the play's timing. This is what you experience early on in your relationship. If you can survive the initial blow, then everything else is a piece of cake. The wide receiver must outwit the defensive back and get to a spot at the right time. The quarterback does not throw the ball to the receiver—he throws it to a spot. The ball has to be released prior to the receiver getting to the spot in order to be a successful play. God has already released your blessing, but you must run your route.

YOU'VE GOT TO BE FAITHFUL
TO THE FINISH LINE

In this season God says, "You've got to be faithful." When you're faithful, you can say with Paul, "I press toward the mark for the prize of the high calling of God in Christ Jesus." I've got to be faithful. I've got to run my race with confidence. Faithfulness comes by faith; it gives you confidence to run to where the ball is going to be thrown so that you'll be ready to receive the blessings God intends for you. And faith comes by hearing, and hearing comes by the Word of God. You wonder why some people are so faithful in spite of all they're going through? You may know couples who have had it rough and wonder how they do it. It's because of what they know. They know the Word of God is what's keeping them hanging in there and keeping them enduring it. And if you will stay faithful to His Word and stay faithful to your assignment, God's promises are going to come to pass. That's why you've got to keep pressing on through your tears,

God's promises will come to pass.

pressing on through your haters, and pressing on through your naysayers.

With every attack of the enemy, God says, "I want you to understand, no matter what comes in your life, you've got to make up in your mind that you've got to finish what you started."

When a couple is focused on destiny, they are not distracted by contrary circumstances. They are motivated to finish everything they start. If you never view life this way on a personal basis, you will never embrace it as a couple. Remember, you are together for more than yourselves. You must persevere and realize that every task is a small part of destiny. God always gives us an anointing for every assignment. To leave something incomplete is an insult to God. Remember, He finished everything He started. We enjoy our relationship with Him today because He declared on the cross, "It is finished."

FINISH THE ASSIGNMENT

There's some of you that don't understand that the prize of the high calling of God is simply the totality of your existence. "God, I have endured what I was supposed to endure and I have finished my assignment. I'm at a point in my life where I want **God to be glorified**; I want the people of **God to be edified**; I want that **devil to be horrified**." I know some of you feel like giving up and

> **When God is *glorified*, I am *edified*, and the devil is *horrified*.**

some of you feel like the race is too tough for you. But I've come to announce that you aren't the first one to go through it and feel like giving up.

- **Jeremiah** felt like giving up one day. He had destiny on his life. He said, "God, I'm tired of doing this. I'm tired of going through what I've got to go through." But Jeremiah came back and said his word was like fire shut up in his bones. He had to finish what he started.
- **Isaiah** was prophesying to people who were disjointed, people who were depressed and felt like giving up. But Isaiah declared to them, "Hast thou not known? hast thou not heard, that the everlasting God . . . giveth power to the faint; and to them that have no might he increaseth strength. Even the youths shall faint and be weary, and the young men shall utterly fall: But they that wait upon the LORD shall renew their strength; they shall mount up with wings as eagles; they shall run, and not be weary; and they shall walk, and not faint" (Isaiah 40:28-31).
- **Job** felt like giving up one day, but he declared, "Though he slay me, yet will I trust in him" (Job 13:15).
- **Jesus** was on the cross one day, had every reason to give up, but He looked up and said, "It is finished!"
- **Quitting is not an option.**

I remember counseling a couple who had been married for over twenty years. They wanted to call it quits. What they had failed to realize was that both of them had changed and there was a lack of communication between them, so they had no way to understand that change. They felt they were at a point of no return and had grown bitter towards each other. Perhaps you are in a relationship and you feel like quitting. What this couple learned is a lesson that should be applied to us all. Hebrews 12:1 says, "Wherefore seeing we [have this] great a cloud of witnesses, . . . let us run with patience the race that is set before us, Looking unto Jesus the author and finisher of our faith."

The **first** lesson was that we are not the first persons to experience difficult times. The **second** lesson is that the same God who pulled others through is able to pull us through. The **third** lesson is that of focus. The couple had taken their eyes off of Jesus and had begun to look at everything that was wrong. They came to realize that they weren't the only couple going through this, so they asked for help. They admitted that they didn't have all the answers. Then they realized that God was there to help them too, not keep account of who did what to whom. Finally, they learned that when their focus falters, it can be fatal. They decided to look to God for encouragement and strength, because the moment they lost focus on Him was the moment that hopelessness set in. Like them, you may have to come to a point that you are willing to fight for your marriage. Fight for what God has ordained for your life.

THE WAY OF DESTINY: YAC'S

In the game of football there are various statistics, and one of those statistics is called YAC. When you see a running back or you see a wide receiver get the ball in their hands, they have one destination in mind—the end zone. But there's opposition on the defensive side. And that defense is determined to stop them from getting to their destiny. But let me tell you what makes a superstar. What makes a superstar is that after he gets hit, he doesn't go down with the first hit but gets **yards after contact—YACs**. He can get hit again and get even more yards.

Maybe you've been hit with disease, you've been hit by being laid off, you've been hit by a negative relationship. Hold on! Look ahead to what the end is going to be, and while you're going, go with your head up, go with your hands up, and give God glory.

But here is the beauty of being a couple—when you get tired, you can throw a lateral pass. You can have your helpmate carry the ball toward the end zone. It's really about working together. There are times when I grow weary from day-to-day work, yet I'm able to draw strength from Stephaine, and vice versa. Now I know you are asking, what do we do when both of us are fatigued and need encouragement? We communicate honestly about where we are and don't project expectations upon each other. We compromise and spend time in prayer asking God to strengthen us for the journey. Until you see yourself as a team, you will never experience this in your relationship.

This is about destiny. It's about how you end up. Why are you here? What's the whole point of it? You're here because God has a plan bigger than most of the folk around you. Some folk look at you and don't understand all the greatness inside of you. But God is so awesome that He kept you from hurt, harm, and danger to preserve you for this moment. "The devil is so stupid! He thought one demon was going to tackle me. But it's going to take more than one demon to bring me down. It's going to take more than one setback. It's going to take more than one doctor's visit. It's

going to take more
than one time being
broke. You don't
know who I am! But
I know who my destiny is!"

> **God has big plans.**

When God brings you together for relationship, He equips you to handle whatever comes your way. Your past experiences were didactic, learning experiences. Your current challenges are preparing you for future challenges. The clearer you see your destiny, the bigger it will become. Once you see your destiny, the smaller your current problems will become. Any threat to destiny will be met with courage, not cowardliness. You are better together than you are apart. Draw strength from each other's gifts and encourage each other to fulfill the God-given destiny that brought you together. You will be amazed at the results.

CHASING DESTINY AS A COUPLE

1. Where do you need to be more patient, with yourself, or with each other?
2. Name at least one thing you do well.
3. Name at least one thing the other person does well.
4. Where do you invest your time? your money? your energy?
5. If you knew you wouldn't fail and had all of heaven behind you, what would you do?
6. Find a verse in the Bible that means a lot to you both.
7. How can you better share the load?

CHAPTER THREE

DATE FOR DESTINY: WE CAN, WE WILL, WE MUST

When you discover your purpose, you can, you will, and you must move into the thing that God has already ordained for your life. God is a God of purpose. Everything that God does, no matter where, when, or how, He does it for a reason. Everything that God does, He does it with purpose, with a design, a plan—bringing order out of our chaos.

Everything that God created, He created with purpose. Purpose then precedes creation. Everything in life begins and ends with purpose. And the best, most successful lives are lived according to God's purpose. That is our destiny, to live exclusively in God's purpose.

Many of us have been blessed by Rick Warren's book *The Purpose Driven Life*. It's a powerful book that reminds us that it's important to understand that all believers must be purpose-driven in everything we do, because God's will is that we live and breathe His purpose.

PURPOSE MAKES YOU SIGNIFICANT

Purpose is the only thing that will give meaning to life and make you significant and relevant to this present generation and generations after you. The aim of life, then, should be to become significant. It would be a tragedy to live your life and then die keeping all that God has deposited in you. Do you want to be significant? Do you want your life to matter? Then you can, you will, and you must keep your date with destiny.

Myles Munroe, in his book *In Pursuit of Purpose*, says: "The greatest tragedy in life is not death, but life without a reason, a purpose. It is dangerous to be alive and not know that reason you are given life. One of the most frustrating experiences is to have time but not know why."

A person I consider a great thinker is Benjamin Mays. He put it this way, "The tragedy of life doesn't lie in not reaching your goal; the tragedy lies in having no goal to reach. It isn't a calamity to die with dreams unfulfilled, but it is a calamity not to dream. It is no disgrace to reach for the stars, but it is a disgrace to have no stars to reach for."

Failure is not a sin, but low aim is. How many people do you know who have such low aim that they miss the totality of what God intends for their lives? But, you ask, what is purpose and why is it so important that I put myself in God's purpose?

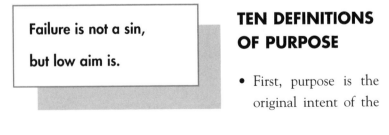

Failure is not a sin, but low aim is.

TEN DEFINITIONS OF PURPOSE

- First, purpose is the original intent of the

creation of a thing. Think about this for a minute. When you make a chocolate cake, you do it with the intent of—for the purpose of—eating it.

- Second, purpose is the original reason for the creation of a thing. The reason cakes were invented in the first place was so that people could eat them.

- Third, purpose is the end for which the means exist. This means in our cake example, we make the cake in a way that will ensure that we can eat it when it's finished. We use ingredients—lots of chocolate—and bake it at 350 degrees for a set period of time, so it will be fit to eat.

- Fourth, purpose is the cause of the thing. So our need to eat chocolate causes us to find ways to satisfy that need, and one way we satisfy our need is by making cakes.

- Fifth, purpose is the desired result that initiates production. We desire to eat chocolate, so we are motivated to begin making the cake.

- Sixth, purpose is the need that makes a manufacturer produce a specific product. We need chocolate, so a manufacturer looks out and sees our need and produces chocolate cakes.

- Seventh, purpose is the destination that prompts the journey. This is my favorite. When I get tired on the journey, it helps me to think about the destination. When I'm hungry and tired, it helps me to think about the end product.

- Eighth, purpose is the aspiration for the inspiration. Why are you so inspired? Because of what I'm aspiring to. I'm aspiring to create a wonderful dessert, and you get inspired to help.

- Ninth, purpose is the object one wills or resolves to have. I resolve that I'm going to make that cake. The cake fulfills my resolve.

  Why am I leading you through Cake Baking 101? Because the tenth definition puts the rest in perspective.

- Tenth, purpose is, then, more than a personal context. It is the original intent in the mind of God that prompted Him to create you. God had an idea in His mind when He created you. God didn't just create you and say, "Now, what am I going to do with you?"

How do we know the mind of God, His purpose? Nobody knows the mind of God, save the Spirit of God, so I can never know my purpose outside of a relationship with God in Christ Jesus. It is a tragedy to try to figure out, navigate my life, and try to discover my purpose without a relationship with God. It is literally impossible. You were created for a purpose, and that purpose is from God. And to know your purpose, you must have an ongoing relationship with God. Want to know your purpose? Get to know God better.

HOW DO I GET MY PURPOSE?

> **God had an idea in His mind when He created you.**

How *do* I get my purpose? After I'm born, I'm subject to all the social influences and all the things of the world. They impact my life and pull me this way and that—

peer pressure, trying to fit in. I don't want to be weird, so I get involved with things—maybe things I shouldn't. At twelve and fourteen, I'm in this; at sixteen, I do that. At eighteen, I'm rebelling. You know, I think I'm grown, so I'm sleeping around. By age twenty-five, I just don't know what's happening in my life. And then all of a sudden, God calls me.

By the way, preachers are not the only people who are called. All Christians are called to follow and live under the mantle of Christ. But how does He do it? He uses His Word to do it. God connects me with a preacher who speaks into my life, and His Word is calling me back to my original intent. So now I start saying, "Okay, I got to stop this. This is not who I am." I start becoming less and less tolerant of what I used to be tolerant of because I feel a call on my life. I might still tip, but it doesn't feel right anymore. I have thoughts, but they don't feel right anymore. I'm under the Word, and that Word is speaking directly to me.

I answer the call and say, "Okay, God, yes. What do you want me to do?" Then God gives it to you and the first thing you say is, "Well, God, wait a minute. You want somebody like me who did all that, to do this? God, I feel so inadequate. God, I'm not sure. How could somebody with my past do that?" Then God tells me, "Listen, the only people I call are imperfect people, because I have nobody else to choose from. Besides, once I call you, I will also justify you." God will equip you. God will give you a clean slate, so whatever you do then, you can give God the credit. Does this make you lucky? No, it makes you blessed and

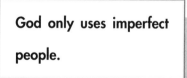

God only uses imperfect people.

blessed by God. Luck is playing the lottery, where the odds are all against you. Being blessed by God means that you have a one-hundred-percent chance of winning.

BE A PLAYER

God saves you for a purpose. He gives you an assignment. He equips you to run the race. He empowers you so that you can advance the ball many yards after contact. Be a player in your own life; don't procrastinate. Seize your moment now.

I know when I refer to being a player, many of you cringe. I am not referring to being a player in the sense of violating trust and covenant. I am using this term as a term of accountability and responsibility for your future. You cannot wait for others to do for you what God has empowered you to do for yourself.

One of the things I appreciate about my wife is that, prior to our meeting, she had accomplished so much. She pursued her dreams and became incredibly successful in her own right. She did not sit around and wait for a knight in shining armor to come and take care of her. She did a pretty good job taking care of that herself. When we came together we came to complement each other.

This is the wonderful thing about people who seize their moment. They don't go through life bitter with unmet expectations. I see so many couples who experience this and engage in the blame game. One person in the relationship feels they would have advanced further in their career if they had not given up so much for the relationship. Relationships rooted in destiny add value. They do not make you worse off. I will say it again. This is your moment and you must be willing to achieve your goals as an individual, and this spirit of determination will spill over into your relationship.

You are God's product. And only God has the right to determine what your destiny should be, not you or any other person.

TEN THINGS YOU NEED TO KNOW ABOUT PURPOSE

There are ten things people need to understand about their date with destiny.

- **One.** God is the source of your purpose. In Him is your destiny best fulfilled. Philippians 1:6 says (my paraphrase), "He who has started a good thing in you will complete it." He will finish it. He will complete it.
- **Two.** Purpose is predetermined. Second Timothy 1:9, "[He] saved us, and called us with an holy calling, not according to our works, but according to his own purpose." It's God's purpose. So it's predetermined. Jeremiah 1:5 says, "Before I formed [you] . . . , I knew [you]." In Matthew 10:30, He says, "I know every hair on your head—or the lack thereof."
- **Three.** My purpose is an integral part of who I am. God takes everything into consideration: how He made me, my idiosyncrasies, my character, my personality, my sense of humor, everything. When I was a young boy, I had a lot of energy, like I had ADHD. We'd have a hundred-yard dash, I'd run two hundred yards. I was never sent out of class, but I was always active, always talking, looking for something to get into. I was just a hyper, hyper, hyper kid, hyper, hyper, hyper, hyper. And they would test me for special education;

they thought something was wrong with me, but I passed the test. I did. But that's because I had my mother, who believed in me. She'd say, "He's not special; he's gifted." And that's what they found out: I was gifted; I just had so much energy.

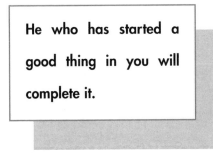

He who has started a good thing in you will complete it.

My whole life there's been all this energy. It's still there today. I get up and preach five services on Sunday, and I get up at 5:00 in the morning. At 4:30 in the morning I go to the gym and play basketball. I've got energy; I'm just like that. I don't drink all those drinks; I just have natural energy. Wonder why God would give me that? Because my purpose is an integral part of who I am. I mean, who else would He have pastor the church, running around town?

See, folks show up to mid-week Bible study, come draggin' in. I know they are, like, "Oh, it's seven o'clock is too late for a Bible study. I'll miss my TV show." Others get off work, go to the gym, and then come out. But I've been preaching all day—twelve, five, and seven p.m. You see? On Sunday, it's seven, eight-fifteen, nine-thirty, eleven a.m. Then it's five o'clock in the morning again. But it doesn't bother me, because this is my assignment.

That's why you got to know what your assignment is, because people will always say, "I want you to do this, this, and this." So if you don't have an anointing for your assignment, you gonna hurt yourself doing all this. You may love children—that's why you teach. You're patient. If you don't love children, why do you want to teach? I know pastors who don't like people, but they want to pastor. I'm like, "You don't like people, man. Go preach, go be an evangelist, travel the world, stop being a pastor and making folk mad." 'Cause it's an integral part of who you are. God takes all that into consideration.

- **Four.** Your purpose is a solution to a problem. In Exodus 3:7 God sees the problem. What's the problem? "My children are being oppressed." The Israelites are in bondage and He hears their cry. In verse 8 and verse 9, God says, "I heard them; I saw their oppression. I saw them; I heard them." That's the problem. So God called Moses to solve the problem.

- **Five.** Your purpose is for a person or a people. Always. God never gives you a purpose just for yourself. It's always for a person or a people. In Exodus 3:10 God says to Moses, "OK, I'm getting ready to send you to Pharaoh, that you may bring my people, the children of Israel, out of Egypt."

- **Six.** Your purpose is your assignment. Assignments are to be finished and not

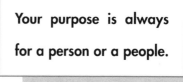

Your purpose is always for a person or a people.

ished and not merely started and left incomplete. In Isaiah 6:8, when Isaiah saw the Lord high and lifted up, the Lord said to him, "Well then, who shall I send? Who will go for us?" And Isaiah said, "Here am I, send me." This is my assignment. I know my assignment—I'm clear.

- **Seven.** Your purpose determines your destiny. **Purpose is the path to a destiny.** When I get in my purpose, my life ends up how I got in my purpose. In Genesis 12:1-2, the Bible says this (my paraphrase), "The Lord said to Abram, 'Get out of your country, from your kinfolk, from your father's house, into a land that I will show you.' " Go get into purpose; watch this. Here's destiny. This is how your life is going to end up, Abram, if you do this, "I'm going to make you a great nation and I'm going to bless you and I'm going to make your name great and you shall be a blessing." Because you got into your purpose. This is your destiny. The decisions you make determine your destiny.

- **Eight.** But also your purpose is interrelated. It literally impacts the lives of other people, because in Genesis 12:3, He says (my paraphrase), "I will bless them that bless you, and I will curse them that curse you, and in you shall all the families of the earth be blessed." Because you got in line with your purpose, other people are gonna be blessed. Can you imagine what happens if you don't walk in your purpose? How many people will miss out on what God intends for their lives through you? There are people you haven't even met yet who are gonna be blessed by you walking in your purpose.

  Think about seventeen years ago, before I started pastoring—seventeen years ago in your life, think about it. If I had gone to law school and said, "Lord, I don't want to preach," chances are that you probably wouldn't be reading this book right now. What God did in my life blesses you. And consequently, when you decide to say "Yes" to God's purpose, somebody will be blessed fifteen years from now.

- **Nine.** Your purpose stimulates passion. Passion, passion, passion. Feel your passion. Look at 2

> **Purpose is the path to a destiny.**

Corinthians 4:1-7. Study it closely. "Therefore seeing we have this ministry, as we have received mercy, we faint not." We're not tired; we have passion for this. For me there's not been one day since I've pastored Mt. Zion, there's not been one Sunday, one Wednesday, when I have dreaded coming to church. I am so passionate. I get up early and realize I still got another hour before I have to go to worship. Oh, it's not time yet? You want to know why? Because I'm passionate. People look and say, "How do you do that, man?" Because I'm passionate about it. You give me a Bible, you give me an opportunity to teach, I can talk to you all day long. Because what? This is my passion. I love it, I get geeked for it, I mean I'm like, whoo, I just can't wait to do this now.

If you go to your job and you're like, "Oh, Lord Jesus. Father, give me the strength," it's a good indication you are not in your purpose. If you go to work and you're like, "Whooo yeah, but it's on now! It's on now!" You may laugh, but you see my point.

- **Ten.** Purpose transcends pain. This is a hard one, because what pain does is focus your attention on the hurt. This can be a good thing. When you scrape your knee, you need to pay attention, so the wound doesn't get infected. There are proper steps you need to do to take care of yourself. In this sense the pain is a gift from God, because it is a part of the healing process.

But sometimes the pain triggers other things and opens old wounds. Sometimes we just can't seem to get beyond it. There might be flashbacks, nightmares, destructive thoughts tempting us to yield to destructive behaviors. How can we get past this complicated kind of pain, a pain that, instead of being part of the healing process, becomes destructive. This kind of pain feeds on itself, and it threatens to suck the life out of us. Here we need the strength to call for help, because this kind of pain ensnares us and binds us so that we sometimes can't even move. What happens then?

The Apostle Paul had this kind of pain. He called it a thorn in his flesh, and he asked God repeatedly to remove it, and God didn't. God told him that, "My grace is sufficient for you." And Paul says, "Well then, I will then glory in my infirmities that the power of Christ may rest upon me." I'm just gonna give God glory, I'm gonna transcend the pain. God's help will keep you in your purpose.

Often when we experience crisis, we lose sight of purpose. I remember experiencing my own "thorn" a few years ago. I began to ask God, Why me? I struggled with God for a while, only to discover that while I was struggling, He was sustaining me. I was speaking around the world and yet hurting. I was encouraging other people, yet I was falling apart myself. God had to remind me that my calling was greater than my crisis. He reminded me that my purpose was greater than my problems and that my destiny was greater than my dilemma. No longer could I take what I was going through personally. As you read this book, begin to think about the awesome destiny ahead of you. Once you do that, you can rise above anything you are going through and come to a place of peace, knowing this: He will never lead me where His grace cannot sustain me.

GOD'S HAND IS UPON YOU AS A COUPLE

Everything you've read in this chapter so far speaks primarily to individuals first, because healthy relationships are made up of healthy individuals. A Christ-centered relationship for a couple is possible only when both persons are walking in God's purpose toward their destiny. But God also knows that walking in His purpose requires companionship. So He wants to bless you as a couple as well, and He has a purpose in mind for you as a couple that you cannot achieve alone.

That's the beauty of coming together with the right person. You recognize that there is joint vision and joint destiny. You must move from "me" to "we." Whenever God gives vision, He always involves people who can run with it. I found myself a widower for three years with so much God wanted to do in my life. What I discovered is that I needed partnership to share in the vision with me. Stephaine and I are partners for life because we embrace and affirm what God is doing in both of our lives. We have seen first-hand how God has used our lives together for His glory.

I remember going to the hospital to visit a family who was in crisis. A family member was quite ill, and it didn't look like he would make it through the night. I was accustomed to praying and encouraging families in crisis situations, because I had done it so many times before. It was a pleasant surprise to see Stephaine share with the family from a personal and professional level to bring comfort in areas where I could not.

This was just one example among many where God has confirmed His hand upon us as a couple. He uses us to bless people. Because we are committed to His will for our lives, we recognize that our destiny is unfolding every day. My friend Bishop Lester Love inspired the phrase I have used in this chapter, "I can, I will, and I must." With God's hand upon your life as a couple, you can make it. You will make it together; and considering the destiny ahead of you, you must make it.

WE CAN, WE WILL, WE MUST AS A COUPLE

1. In your relationship, who is the quarterback, the forward, the clean-up batter?

2. Take some time and set two goals to do as a couple. For example, set apart more time for each other; make a budget and stick to it; plan a big trip; invite some Christian friends to dinner; attend church together; and so on.

3. Talk about your dreams for the future. Then start mapping out a way to make those dreams a reality.

4. Discuss the hardships you've endured together.

5. On a scale of one to ten (one being low and ten being high), how well do you listen to each other?

6. On a scale of one to ten (one being low and ten being high), how patient are you with each other?

7. Promise to find ways to praise each other and celebrate your achievements.

8. How do you see God's hand on you as individuals and as a couple?

CHAPTER FOUR

DESTINY ON PURPOSE: DEFINING MOMENTS

I have to admit that I am amazed at how God providentially brought Stephaine and me together. How could a boy reared in Shreveport, Louisiana, connect with a girl from Los Angeles, California? It is simple. Our steps were ordered by the Lord. My purpose was set before the foundations of the world, and God knew how my life would evolve. One of the most important lessons for any of us to remember is that nothing just happens. Every experience in our childhood is a part of the larger puzzle. Every failure and success was a part of the molding process. It is important to embrace your journey because it does have a destination.

Stephaine and I had very similar childhoods because our homes were very similar. Our parents shared the same values and struggles, and it has kept us grounded even today. I never shall forget when our parents met for the first time. It was not only a first time for them, but neither had Stephaine's parents met me nor had my parents met her. I must admit, I had a great deal of anxiety about this moment; but when it occurred, it was like a family reunion. Things just clicked. When you are destined to be together, these things become easy. We were created for this moment.

Whether or not you acknowledge you are God's child; you are part of God's family; God created you. He created you *in* His image and *for* His purpose. Even if you don't understand why God has put you where you are, even if you don't understand the real reason you got together as a couple, God does. God is in control. But there are defining moments that can solidify your place in God's kingdom. These are the moments when you choose to live in God's purpose or apart from it.

And you are also a product of your environment. When you were born really had nothing to do with you. You were born into sin, and you really didn't have anything to do with that, either, thanks to Adam and Eve. Because you were born into sin, you were born into this flesh with no concept of purpose and your true identity. It was in infancy, then, when you began to be bombarded with certain cultural realities—your mom and dad were together, they were divorced, they were somewhere in-between—your house was roomy, it was cramped with one bathroom, it was something in-between. You had a difficult life; you had an easy life; but more likely, it was something in-between.

You were raised in church or you weren't. But however you were raised, ultimately all of us become a product of the things that we take to be normal and natural, like the air we breathe. We don't question why, we just accept them as what is. So you come along and you grow and you really know God, you know there is a God. Perhaps you grow up in an ungodly house. You've never heard of God and could care less. In either case, you eventually accept the Lord Jesus Christ as your personal Savior and you become saved. Your old self—all those influences that were inconsistent with the original plan of God for your life—is dead to you.

BE FREE TO LOVE

The whole concept of salvation says that something in you should have died. What needs to die? All those things that keep you away from God—all the influences in your life that are inconsistent with God's original plan for your life. Do you want to know what God's original plan for you was? Do you want to know who God thought of when He first thought of you? He thought of Jesus—His child. That might surprise you a little, but it's true. When I think about the kind of person Jesus is, I can't think of anyone I'd rather have as a friend or a person I'd rather be like.

Once you are saved, you are now turned toward God. That's regeneration. It means that I'm going somewhere; I'm born again; I get to start over. So there was one birthday my momma told me about, but another birthday I told her about. What happens now? I turn my focus to God. For the first time in my life, now I am pursuing a relationship with God for me. Not because someone is making me go to church, not because my family says this is what we do or we're gonna be this—it's personal.

> **All those things that keep you away from God interfere with God's original plan for your life.**

> **When God is in the center of me, my own self-centeredness is gone.**

But I don't chase God just for my own well-being, for myself, because my personal relationship with God also benefits everyone I know, and it benefits the people who are closest and most intimate to me the most. **When God is in the center of me and my own self-centeredness is gone, I am truly free to love and give and receive love out of His great reservoir of grace; because it's literally in me to give freely.**

TO CHASE PURPOSE, CHASE GOD

You ask, "Walker, man, why are you talking about this?" Because before I can chase the purpose, I have to chase God. I've got to have Him first. That's why the Bible says, "Seek ye first the kingdom of God, and his righteousness; and all these things shall be added unto you" (Matthew 6:33). But even if you are chasing after God, please understand that God is always chasing you. That is what grace is all about.

Once I'm in this salvation process, once I walk into this relationship with God, God drops something in my spirit. He says, "THIS is what you're supposed to do. THIS is who you are supposed to be with. THIS is how you are to live your life." It's in my spirit.

But now I may have a problem. What God drops in my spirit often challenges all the stuff I've been raised believing that I was supposed to be. So now I have to begin to confront my situation and ask: Am I going to go back and challenge all the stuff everybody said I ought to be, or am I gonna chase the thing that God said I was originally designed to be?

I thought I was going to be a lawyer; look at me now—a preacher. I had my heart set on being an attorney, but I remember my late grandmother saying to me that the purpose of God brings peace. I have a friend who we will call Mike. Mike was convinced that he was going to be an entertainer, yet he never had peace. We played in the same bands together and shared a mutual interest in music; however, it was clear it was a hobby, not a passion. Mike took a special interest in special needs children. He would always talk about what needed to be done to help them and how he would do more when his music career took off. Although everybody was convinced that Mike was on his way to becoming the next big thing in music, those of us close to him knew that this passion of helping special needs kids was growing inside of him. Needless to say, a few years ago Mike graduated from college to pursue a full-time teaching position in a special needs school. Many of us, like Mike, have made up our minds what we think we want to do in life, but the real answer lies in the passion in our hearts.

LORD, YOU WANT ME TO DO *WHAT!?*

Once purpose is made known, the challenge now becomes, "Lord, well,

Everybody that God shows His purpose to will always struggle with it.

then, how in the world does somebody like me step into something like that?" But I want to reassure you that this is normal—everybody that God shows His purpose to will always struggle with it.

- Remember when God called Moses, He said, "This is your purpose; go tell Pharaoh to let My people go." All Moses had was a stick and a stutter, and Moses was like, "Lord, what am I gonna do? How is somebody like me gonna do that?"
- Jeremiah struggled with it. He said, "Lord, I'm too young."
- Jonah said, "God, no, you must have the wrong man."

Anytime purpose is made known to you, it always brings about a certain amount of anxiety and fear. Let me reassure you that your anxiety and fear are perfectly normal. God is in the business of showing us where we are yet to walk. And our fear and anxiety can serve to bring us *closer* to Him. It doesn't have to make us run away and hide. God prepares a place for you; He leads you in paths of righteousness. Psalm 23 also says that, "Surely goodness and mercy shall follow me." This means that not only is God out in front leading the way and blazing the trail, He is also behind you cleaning up the mess you leave behind. Do you get it? God walks in front of you, beside you, and behind you. When you walk in His purpose, God, Himself, is your companion.

> **When you walk in His purpose, God, Himself, is your companion.**

TRUST GOD WITH YOUR DESTINY

So how do I walk in it? Once you've been born again, you are born with a purpose; God sets you on the right path. You respond by following in God's footsteps by reading the Word; being part of God's mission to the least, the last, and the lost; finding Christian friends who share your goals and dreams; living a disciplined life; and growing in love and knowledge. But you say, "Bishop, that's fine for you; but I ain't perfect, and frankly, I don't want to be." But please believe me that if a Christian life is your aim, God will empower you. You may fall off and away, often and hard, but God's ever-seeking love will find a way to bring you back to Him.

Destiny is how I end up. And I don't know about you, but I want to end up with God. Walking in purpose means walking toward what God scripted your end to be. Look at Ephesians 1:11, "In whom also we have obtained an inheritance." We have something great waiting for us. Because we have been predestined "according to the purpose of him who worketh all things after the counsel of his own will." We don't have to be afraid, because God intends only good for us. He offers us a worthy prize.

I have a reward because God predestined my purpose. He set my way before the foundation of the world. What God has in store for you is, in the end, greater than anything you can imagine. Whatever God is allowing to happen in your life, it is all tied to the

> **We aren't afraid because God intends only good for us.**

purpose He originally ordained for your life. That's why you can stop whining about stuff God allows. Say instead, "Well, Lord, if you let that happen, there's got to be a greater purpose for it." So when you're trying to go back and ask God to give your stuff back, remember that maybe He meant for you to lose it. Sometimes God takes stuff away, because there's some things that we're never going to be able to handle if we are going to walk with Him. We just have to trust Him.

GOD KNOWS YOUR NAME

Jeremiah 1:5 says, "Before I formed thee in the belly, I knew thee; and before thou camest forth out of the womb I sanctified thee, and I ordained thee a prophet unto the nations." God knows you, but the devil knows you too. That's why the devil always tries to kill you before the will of God gets manifest in your life. If the devil can take you out before you understand what your purpose is, he can destroy the plan of God that is supposed to happen on this earth. The devil will surround you with dangerous people.

Here is a dangerous person—a person who doesn't know Jesus Christ as their personal savior and who doesn't know their purpose. Because what they do is, they listen to what the devil says they're designed to do. So they live out their lives in an anti-Christ mode—everything, that is, that is against Christ, that's what they do. And there are no two ways about it: a person is either for Christ or against Christ. There is no in-between on this. I would rather be in a relationship with Him and not know my purpose than be out of a relationship with Him and not know my purpose, because I am dangerous. Let me show you how.

On the surface Karen and Tim had a wonderful relationship, but privately they struggled. I remember speaking to Tim and hearing his lamentations about their inability to pinpoint the real issue in the marriage. Karen grew up in a Christian home and went to church regularly. When she met Tim, she didn't go as much. Tim didn't grow up that way and didn't see the need for church or Christ in their marriage relationship. Tim was a brilliant guy, yet he struggled with what to do with himself. He had been in several college programs but never finished. He started several businesses but never followed through on any of them. Tim was privately frustrated and admitted he had no guidance in his life. Karen was frustrated because she was the only source of income in the house. Karen was a nurse and worked long hours; and when she would come home, she and Tim would spend hours fussing.

I shared candidly with Tim that he would never know his purpose outside of Christ and never be the husband God had called him to be until he put things in order. I saw Karen and Tim at a function a year ago and had an opportunity to catch up. Well, Tim apparently took my advice, because his passion for Christ was so obvious it surprised me. I was so pleased to hear he had a personal relationship with Christ. Tim is now finishing his MBA and already has a job lined up. The joy on Karen's face spoke volumes about the importance of aligning purpose and our relationship with Christ.

DEFINING MOMENTS

Are you for or against Christ?

If you get nothing else out of this book,

get this: there is a defining moment when God allows us to see things from His perspective concerning our lives. And it is in those moments we are called to come in agreement with the purpose and God's calling by committing ourselves wholeheartedly to what He desires us to do. *When you do this, you are forcibly laying hold of the destiny that God has marked for each of our lives.* So when that moment comes, when God gives you the opportunity to see your life as He sees your life, you have to instantly latch on to it. You cannot procrastinate. You have to move right on it.

Here is what separates successful people from average people. For successful people, the moment the will of God is made known to them, they instinctively move on it. They don't need your opinion. They don't have to run it by anyone. They just move on it and you have to get the memo later.

I remember when God spoke to me about starting another ministry location. I must admit that, at first, fear gripped me because I didn't want to fail. After much prayer, I began to move on what God said to do. I put together a plan and a team and implemented the vision. I must tell you that God spoke to me during the completion of a $20 million worship facility on one side of town, and before we could complete it, He was speaking to me about another worship center. Statistically there was no support to make it happen. You don't make an investment like that until you are settled into the current location under construction. I had my critics, but I knew what God had said. Today, the other site, our Antioch location is

> **Defining moments are when God allows you to see from His perspective.**

our fastest growing location. I've seen thousands of souls come to Christ in that area. The expansion did not negatively impact the growth on the other campus. You have to know how to trust God even when you doubt yourself.

BEING CHOSEN

First Peter 1:2 says you are the "elect according to the fore-knowledge of God the Father." You are elected by God's vote. You have been chosen through "sanctification of the Spirit." This means that when you are chosen by God, you *automatically* strug-gle with your inadequacies. Remember your old life? God sancti-fied you; He cleaned you up. He looked at all of your issues and said, "I sanctify you." Because of the relationship you have with Jesus Christ, you have been made right with God. This is why you've got to stop letting people make you feel guilty and ashamed of what you're doing for God. If you're walking in pur-pose, you can say, "You know what, it's blowing my mind that I'm doing it. But thank God I've been sanctified in the blood of Jesus." I'm doing it because of God's power—and none of us really qualify to do it.

GET YOUR STUFF OUT OF GOD'S WAY

Once you accept the fact that you are chosen, the next step is to "present your bodies a living sacrifice, holy, acceptable unto God, which is your reasonable service" (Romans 12:1).

In other words, purpose says, "Get yourself out of the way." Stop worrying and say this to God, "God, I want Your will to

> **Don't worry about trying to *fit in*. Purpose will always make you *stand out*.**

show in my life. God, whatever You got to take out of me, take it out—all the pride, all the sin, all the foolishness, all the crazy stuff. Take me as I am, but change me into what you want, because I know it will be for the good."

Don't worry about trying to fit in. The thing about purpose is that it will always make you stand out. Because if you are a conformer, or you've got to be in a place where you look like everybody else and do what everybody else is doing, you will never walk in the way God tells you. Everybody God calls is uniquely called to be different. We all have different calls that lead to unique destinies. This also means that we will think differently and have different opinions. We may even differ in our opinions, but what will hold us together is walking in our differences on the path of God's purpose.

This especially applies to couples. You will never agree on everything because you have different viewpoints and unique destinies. But this does not mean that you have to argue and fight and keep score about who wins. There is a path that God wants you to walk together. Your job is to keep to the plan.

Stephaine and I, admittedly, are strong-willed individuals. We bump heads when our opinions are at stake. We've learned that the solution is not to think about who "wins," but to assure each other that our contribution to the issue is significant. So often, couples play verbal tennis. It's back and forth, trying to score points. You have to come to a place in your relationship where you value differing opinions. You can disagree without conflict. You can walk in God's purpose together even if disagreements occur. I've learned to embrace Stephaine's viewpoint because it forces me to think outside of my comfort zone. I don't view her input as a challenge; rather, I view it as a complement to our destiny. We are confident that we will arrive at destiny more informed because every option was presented before we proceeded down the path of purpose.

GOD WILL PREVAIL

Jesus chose ordinary men and women and took them on an extraordinary journey to live out their purpose. And they did, often with great difficulty—remember Peter's denial and Judas's betrayal. But as Matthew 11:12 tells us, and this is especially clear in the NIV translation, the kingdom of God is forcibly advancing. God's intent in the earthly realm has been, "The bus is moving. The problem is, ain't enough folk getting on the bus." God's agenda isn't just moving forward, it is forcing its way forward through all kinds of stuff—persecution, cynicism, criticism, and sometimes us. **But take comfort; have confidence; God's agenda will always prevail.**

I often see couples stuck in a rut because they refuse to move outside of their comfort zones. You know couples like this who desire more, yet they don't plan or implement. The problem is that couples around them are progressing and they are at a standstill. I've met couples who were friends with other couples; but when dreams were realized, the friendships became strained.

> **God's agenda will always prevail.**

Unmet expectations will bring out insecurities in people. Don't become that couple who covets what God is doing in the life of your friends when you have the same opportunities to achieve. Time waits for no one. You must make things happen. God's agenda will prevail with or without you, but I suspect you want to be on the winning side.

LAY HOLD OF YOUR CLAIM

The kingdom is forcibly advancing. Look to the hills from where cometh our help. Open your windows and doors, because God is pouring out blessing. Our kingdom is not tied to the world's kingdom. Grass withers; flowers fade; heaven and earth will pass away. I don't preach for exercise; you don't just live for now. This Word will last forever.

But because the kingdom advances with or without us, we have to be willing to lay hold to it. Once God reveals it to you, let 'em call you crazy; let 'em call you a fool. If you lay hold to your purpose, God will raise you up and God will do things through you that you never could have imagined. Do you remember David in 1 Samuel 17:20-58? David saw God's perspective in purpose, and his heart was filled with faith as he forcibly took action. Remember when young David had to fight the giant Goliath? When nobody else wanted to go up against Goliath, David realized, "Wait a minute, this must be my turn." Sometimes that's what God will do. He'll put you in a situation and that's why you can't be thinking, "Whoa, wait a minute, now. I'm just a little ol' man and this is a big ol' giant; he's got weapons. He's got big weapons, and all I got is this slingshot."

Here is Goliath. You can hear his armor clinking from miles away. He towers over every other person. He is big. He is armed. And he's mad. And then, here is David—a kid still in school who looks after sheep in his spare time. David's got nothing but his homemade slingshot. The giant looks down his nose at David and asks him, "Who are you to come to me? Who are you to come to Goliath with this?" And David looks at that giant squarely in the eye when he steps out in faith and purpose and answers, "You come to me with your weapons of war? You come to me with your sword? I come to you in the name of the Lord. I come to you in Him who has called me." David's saying, "I may not have the resources you have, but I sure got the backing you don't."

Understand this for your own life. You don't have to make as much as other folks. You don't have to drive the certain kind of car they have. You don't have to have the connections they have. But God will give you the backing because if God be for you, He's more than the whole world is against you.

But don't be fooled. God had prepared David. David had already fought the bear. So ask yourself, "Where have I been?" How has God prepared you? Where were you before you were saved? What life experience have you had? If you're like most folks, you've had good and bad, positive and negative experiences. But no matter what you've done or where you've been, all your experiences were laced with purpose.

REMEMBER GOD HAS BROUGHT YOU THIS FAR

When you walk in purpose, you have to remember that you've come through the wilderness to this side of heaven. But remember significant people, events, circumstances, relationships, jobs, schooling, locations, churches, mentors, families—all who hate you and all who love you—all of these things play a role in your pattern of development that could be the key to you unlocking your destiny. All of it, every mistake, every success, that stuff that you are bitter over, turn it around and let it bless you. Because if you really ponder your history, you can say, "Then, God, why did you allow that to happen to me? There are some things you could have prevented. But you allowed certain things to happen."

I have several friends who were relocated because of Hurricane Katrina. Rather than complain about what they lost, they used it as an opportunity for expansion. One of them started a church in Houston, Texas, and now has a thriving ministry in the area. Not only that, but he recently started services again in New Orleans, so there is one church in two states. What an amazing story of adaptation. I know countless others, but the lessons are all the same. Your history is significant because it propels you into your destiny. You are not a victim, you are a victor. I will say it again. If God allowed it, it is going to bless you.

If I'm going to unlock my destiny, I have to understand that the future is best informed by the past, but not limited by the past. The Bible says in Romans 1:17, "For therein is the righteousness of God revealed from faith to faith, [from experience to experience]: as it is written, The just shall live by faith."

Go get your future!

YOUR DEFINING MOMENTS AS A COUPLE

1. Think about your commitment to each other. Is your commitment to each other growing?

2. How do you as a couple put and keep God at the center of your relationship?

3. Talk about what you really need from each other.

4. Make a renewed commitment to pray together. If you are uncomfortable, start simple. Here is a sample prayer.

> Dear God, You are the King of the universe, and we are committed to serving You by loving each other. Bless our home. Let us be a blessing to everybody who knows us. Guide and protect us, so that one day we will feast at Your heavenly banquet table. In Jesus' name, Amen.

5. What words of encouragement can you give each other today?

6. Promise that next time you disagree, you will listen more and talk less.

7. Keep a list of people you need to pray for.

8. Talk about how you can better share each other's burdens.

CHAPTER FIVE

DESTINY: DON'T SIT ON IT

So far we've talked about the fact that God has placed the promise of greatness inside of you as individuals and as a couple. Despite where you've been or what you've done, God has a destiny in mind for you. Through your hardships and pain, you've been qualified for your date with destiny. But not only has God placed His promise inside of you, His hand is upon you—molding you, shaping you, guiding you, keeping on the pressure to make you strong and worthy. God has so much invested in you because He loves you. To Him you are finer than gold. So who wouldn't want to chase after that?

God positions you. You respond by keeping a watchful and faithful eye on the prize. We respond by moving forward, looking to take and then finish our assignment from God. Yes, there will be struggles, but as we walk in purpose, God empowers us. He strengthens us; He meets us in our mess and then cleans us up so that we're ready and fit to meet life head-on. These things we can, we will, and we must do as we aim high. Even when we get scared and think we can't do it, God can give us power to focus and keep our passion.

What does walking in God's purpose toward our destiny do for us? It makes us truly free to love, to achieve, to have the finest companionship available—His. This is our defining moment, when we have to trust God, the God who knows us even before we're born, the God who will prevail, the God who has brought us this far. All we have to do is grasp our future and walk on to our destiny.

PLAY TIME IS OVER

One question that every person has to face is, *What am I going to do with my life?* You know, we ask little children that question all the time. "What do you want to be when you grow up?" And we smile and nod when they say, "I want to play basketball" or "I want to be a famous movie star." Well, there are many adults who are *still* trying to answer that question. Perhaps you are one of them. In any case, it should be clear that "nothing" is **not** the answer. Because when God created you, He made you for something bigger than you. Your destiny is literally connected to a heavenly design—a design that involves all of creation. And every decision you make could ultimately impact your future.

CHOICES, DECISIONS, CONSEQUENCES

Every day when you wake up, these three things should come to your spirit: choices, decisions, and consequences. The devil takes pleasure in keeping you confused about who you are. That's why you are tempted to sit on it or

> **Why am I here?**

stray from your true purpose. If you are confused about **who** you are, you will never tap into **whose** you are. And you'll

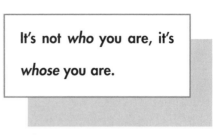

It's not *who* you are, it's *whose* you are.

never be where He wants you to be.

God's desire is for you to be in His will, walking His path toward your destiny. The devil's desire is to keep you out of God's will, because if he can keep you confused, you'll never realize the design that God has for your life and what happens is that you'll end up frustrated, fatigued, and worn out. You may be going through a lot of motion, but you're not moving forward.

IRON SHARPENS IRON: GET A MENTOR

To keep moving forward: this is why every person needs a mentor. Men need mentors; women need mentors. Iron sharpens iron. You need somebody in your life who pushes you and challenges you to explore the greatness that God has placed in your life. It's so easy to find trifling folk, 'cause the devil always plants folk that aren't going anywhere. These folks help keep you comfortable and accepting the apathy in your life. They won't challenge you to go to the next level. But whenever you encounter people in your life who challenge you to go to the next level, you know these relationships are of God. Please understand that they are not going to agree with everything you do, but they're going to challenge you. They are going to say, "Look, there is a better way. God has more for your life."

You need a mentor; you need somebody living this faith out to help you along the path. This mentor is like a coach, somebody who can literally say to you, "I refuse to let you settle for anything beneath your potential." This is the kind of relationship we see in 2 Timothy 1:5-9.

> When I call to remembrance the unfeigned faith that is in thee, which dwelt first in thy grandmother Lois, and thy mother Eunice; and I am persuaded that in thee also. Wherefore I put thee in remembrance that thou stir up the gift of God, which is in thee by the putting on of my hands. For God hath not given us the spirit of fear; but of power, and of love, and of a sound mind. Be not thou therefore ashamed of the testimony of our Lord, nor of me his prisoner: but be thou partaker of the afflictions of the gospel according to the power of God; who hath saved us, and called us with an holy calling, not according to our works, but according to his own purpose and grace, which was given us in Christ Jesus before the world began.

In this scripture we see that Paul is coaching Timothy. Paul is mentoring Timothy, helping him understand some valuable wisdom principles, helping him understand that God has placed greatness inside of him.

As a couple, you also should have another couple to mentor you. A mentor couple should be persons you both admire, people who have a successful relationship and who can help you through rough times. A mentoring couple should be a blessing to those who know them and should continue to grow in Christian love and commitment. If you need suggestions about who would make a great mentor, contact your pastor.

GOD HAS INTEREST IN YOU

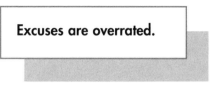

Excuses are overrated.

There are things God is trying to get out of you, so if you're going to be successful, you're going to have to walk into the destiny that God has ordained for your life. You can't sit on it. You can't make excuses. If you are caught in a perpetual state of "fittna," you're "fittna" to do this and "fittna" to do that, it's time now for you to stop making excuses as to why you can't be where God wants you to be and do what God wants you to do.

Whenever somebody makes a deposit, they want some interest on that deposit. God said, "I put too much in you and this deposit is not going to go bad. I want to get everything out of you that I put inside of you." Make up your mind and do what God wants. Even if it means I have to walk by myself, I know there is destiny on my life; there is greatness on my life. If folk don't understand it I am not going to sit another day.

GENERATIONAL GREATNESS

Paul tells Timothy and us some things God wants to get out of us. How do we get them out? To get them out, we first have to understand that there is generational greatness in us. First thing Paul tells Timothy is that your legacy is one of great faith. In a real sense you have no excuses not to succeed because greatness is in your bloodline. That's why it's so important for you to have a pattern, a pattern as a couple and a family.

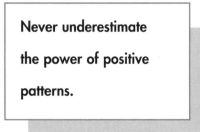

Never underestimate the power of positive patterns.

Paul tells Timothy, "Look, man, your grand-momma, Lois, and your momma, Eunice, they were patterns of faith." Historically, Timothy's father was a Greek and his father forbade him to be circumcised. This limited Timothy and did not allow him to participate in the normal religious routine of the Jewish religion. But his mother and grandmother taught him the Hebrew Scriptures, and as a result of their teaching, he came to know God for himself. Understand, there was greatness in his momma and his grandmomma. This is what Paul is telling Timothy: "There is greatness in you."

Never underestimate the power of a positive pattern in your life. This greatness is a result of these positive patterns, which are the result of positive relationships. We are not here alone, by our-selves. Somebody prayed for you. Somebody kept praying for you. Hebrews 12:1 says, "Wherefore seeing we also [have this great] cloud of witnesses, . . . let us run with patience the race that is set before us, looking unto Jesus the author and finisher of our faith." The Bible tells us that we have all these faithful people who give us a pattern. From them we can see that, by what they've been through, we can make it too.

Thank God for the generational greatness in your life, because someone taught you how to pray when times get tough. Some of us know that when we were out in the world acting like a fool, had it not been for our grandmomma praying or a granddaddy or uncle or somebody who was on their face praying for us, we wouldn't be where we are today. Somebody taught you how to trust God when things got rough. Somebody gave you your first drug problem—that is, they drug you to church. Somebody in your family taught you that when your money gets funny and your change gets strange, you ain't gotta give up, you ain't gotta commit suicide. They taught you how to rub two nickels together. Don't act like you always ate chicken breasts. You've had the back, or wing, and probably a leg too.

THE POWER OF POSITIVE PATTERN

When you understand the power of a positive pattern, then you'll be determined to make certain it gets passed down. Because greatness to the next generation depends on what you are going to do, whether or not you know it. Whatever you're doing now, you're gonna pass down. Statistics teach us children of abusers become abusers themselves. Children of alcoholics have a higher probability of becoming alcoholics. Children who come out of divorced households have a greater chance of being divorced themselves. How you live matters for you and for the next generation.

How you treat your husband or your wife, how you act as a couple will be passed down. You can't sit on it, because our sons and our daughters are looking. And many of us are passing down curses rather than blessings. We have a choice: either we're gonna pass out a blessing or we're gonna pass down a curse. We have a choice. That's why you have to ask yourself when you make choices, "Do I want to pass this down?" Look at it, brother, I'm talking to you, ask yourself, "Do you treat women like objects of your desire?" Ain't nothing to you; so one day when your daughter grows up, be forewarned when she says, "Daddy, meet my new boyfriend! He's just like you!"

> **What are you passing down?**

When you have disagreements as a couple, do you calmly discuss options or do you yell and scream? How you act toward each other is what your kids are going to think is normal. They'll think, "All that? Oh, that's how everybody acts."

When things get rough, do you run **from** God? Or do you run **to** God? When you're struggling financially, do you work your way out of debt and pass down a blessing? Because the Bible says, "A good man leaves an inheritance to his children's children and his grandchildren." Or do you make excuses, living in debt and always hitting folk up? There's too much greatness in you to sit on it and not pass down a blessing to the next generation.

BLESSED TO BE A BLESSING

Everyone around you is supposed to be blessed through you. Your children are supposed to be blessed because you're a blessed man or woman. "Blessed is the man that walketh not in the counsel of the ungodly, nor standeth in the way of sinners, nor sitteth in the seat of the scornful. But his delight is in the law of the LORD; and in his law doth he meditate day and night. And he shall be like a tree planted by the rivers of water, that bringeth forth his fruit in his season; his leaf also shall not wither; and whatsoever he doeth shall prosper" (Psalm 1:1-3). When you are a blessed man, your children are gonna be blessed, your grandchildren are gonna be blessed, your dog's gonna be blessed, your cat's gonna be blessed, your fish is gonna be blessed, everything around you is going to be blessed.

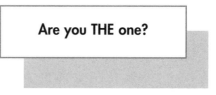

Are you THE one?

There are young men looking right now, searching, saying, "Is there one? Is there one man I can look up to who takes care of his family? Is there one? Is there one man who I can look up to who loves his wife like she's supposed to be loved?" There is some young girl watching you, asking, "Is there one woman who's not the average girl from the video? Her value is not determined by the price of her clothes? Is there one woman who doesn't have to drop it like it's hot or let it down like its warm?" There are young people watching and asking, "Is there any brother who's got a legitimate child? Who's driving a car that they really can afford and living in a nice house and didn't have to sell drugs to do it? Is there one?"

This is real. So tired of all these folk walking around like you a pimp, talking like you a player, walking around being a punk? Be a man! Guys are always whining about something, sitting up in the barbershop gossiping more than a woman! Be a man and handle your business! If you want to be treated like a man, be a man!

GOD GIVES GIFTS

Paul tells Timothy, "This is greatness." You don't have an excuse. There's no reason you can't make it. You can't blame anyone. What you're looking for is not out there, it's already in you. Paul says, "Gifts have been given to you." First, there is power in a positive pattern. Second, God has endowed you with gifts.

The source of these gifts is God, because every good and perfect gift comes from above. So whether or not you know it, you're gifted. And when God gives gifts, these gifts have purpose. He doesn't give gifts without purpose, without direction, without order. So if He gives you a gift, that gift has a purpose, a distinct purpose. If you have trouble seeing your gifts, that's another reason to find a mentor.

STIR IT UP!

Your purpose is like a flame that won't go out. It's that thing you're most passionate about. It's the thing you keep dreaming about. It's that thing you keep saying, "I'm gonna get around to that when I get some free time." Your purpose is that thing that keeps you going. When you get into your purpose, you'll never work another day in your life. Purpose is passion; passion is purpose. When you see a person in purpose, they can just go and do. People look at me and say, "How do you preach all of these services every Sunday, every week?" Because I'm in purpose.

But purpose is also more than passion. Passion gone wild can lead you to jump off a cliff. Passion has to be reined in. Think of it this way: a wild horse only wrecks things and is dangerous to anybody who tries to ride him. A crazy horse can literally run off a cliff and take you with him. It's only after that wild horse gets used to the bridle and learns to respect the reins that he is a thing of beauty. He then knows how to use his strength and run a good race. I don't know anything about Horse Whisperers or how they train a horse, but I do know that once that horse's passion is reined in, only then is he fit to win.

If you are in your purpose, you'll say, "See, I don't mind, because this is what I was put on earth to do." 'Cause when you understand what you were put on earth to do, then you do it knowing this is my purpose; this is my passion. When I understand this, Paul tells Timothy, "This thing that has been put in you I declare to you now, 'Stir it up!' "

As long as you let your gift sit, you run the risk of postponing your purpose. So it's time to get this thing out of your head and put it in your hand. Too much has been invested in you, and God has His hand on you. You don't have to be afraid and you don't need to procrastinate. You got to stir it up, but know that when you start stirring, there'll be agitation. That's why when you stir your gift up, some folk are not going to understand. It's going to make some folk uneasy around you. They're not going to know how to deal with you, because they're not going to be able to control you anymore; it's going to agitate them, but that's all right. You've got to stir this gift up until what God promised you comes to pass.

When you start stirring, it's going to affect all those around you. It's going to affect your friends and your family. It's going to affect your life as a couple. As I mentioned earlier, Stephaine and I understand our gifts and how they work to bless the lives of others. It is important to sit with your significant other and evaluate your gifts together. There should be a common thread that connects your destiny to each other. Once your purpose is discovered and aligned with each other and with God, it focuses

> **As long as your gift sits, you postpone your purpose.**

the relationship beyond itself. No longer does your gift become self-serving; rather, it becomes a conduit by which God blesses the lives of people around the world. When you stir up that gift, it will inspire and motivate those around you. People should be energized when they see your relationship. They should be inspired by your pursuit of greatness. Each day Stephaine and I wake up, we ask God to use us as an example so that others will move closer to their destiny. It's not always easy, but if you are determined, you will do the things that are necessary to achieve your goals.

But you also have to be discerning about your gift. That is another reason to talk to a mentor or your pastor. There was once a woman who had five children. One afternoon, she went to her pastor and told him that she had a call to use her gift from God to be a missionary. And naturally, she wanted to leave immediately and go straight where she'd be needed most—in Africa. The pastor asked her what she planned to do with her children, who, all things considered, were also gifts from God. "Well," she said, "I'm not sure where they're called to." Now, do you think God wanted this woman to stir up her gift and dissolve her family? It's safe to say, probably not. Stirring up your gift may bring agitation, but it is not meant to be used as a weapon to destroy the goodness in your life. And stirring is not meant as an excuse to make trouble.

WHAT'S LOVE GOT TO DO WITH IT?

Love means that when I walk out in this gift, I'm gonna have some people who are going to hate me. Because when gift and purpose get in place, you are an incredibly blessed individual. So people around you are going to hate you like never before, but you've got to love them

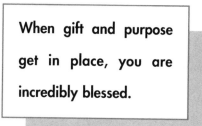

When gift and purpose get in place, you are incredibly blessed.

anyhow. You've got to say, "Look, I don't have time to sit back and let you discourage my purpose and my dreams. I'm just gonna love you anyhow. You don't have to understand, you can bring all the hell you want to in my life, but I'll love the hell out of you. I understand that I have to love you anyhow because of what God is doing in my life."

God, you have not given us the spirit of fear, you have given us love and a sound mind. How does it relate to my gift and my purpose? Because when you step out, when you truly step out into purpose, people are going to look at you and say, "You're crazy." The devil is going to interrogate you, and he's going to say, "What do you think you're trying to do?" And you've got to say, "I've got a sound mind. I'm not crazy, I know I look crazy to you. I'm stepping out on this, but I'm not crazy, because I know what God promised me."

I wish you could've been there the day I got called to preach and the day I said yes to God. There was a good period between the day I got called and the day I said yes; there was a long period from when I said yes to when I said, "Lord, I'll go." I wish you could have heard the devil when he came to me and said, "Ha! Ha! Ha! What are you gonna do? Who's gonna listen to you? You're crazy! You need to go to law school, boy; you don't have any word in you!" That's what the devil tried to tell me, but God kept me with a sound mind; and God didn't allow that devil to mess up my mind because I knew I was called.

When you know you have purpose and destiny on your life, you've got to say, "Lord, keep my mind. Lord, people think I'm crazy, but I know I'm not crazy. I'm gonna do what you called me to do, but people don't understand you when they can't put you in a box." Whenever people cannot put you in a box, they can't control you. They begin to think you've lost your mind. Just have the audacity to believe that you can do what has never been done before. Call me crazy; I just realize that if no one in my family had ever done it before, I was going to be the first one. I was born for this moment.

DO IT FOR GOD'S GLORY

Paul tells Timothy, "Remember this: whatever you do, God's got to get the glory." Because whatever God does through us is ultimately for His glory. That is the original intent of your gift. This is why the devil fights it so. Paul also tells Timothy that persecutions will come, but you can't be ashamed when it happens.

You cannot be ashamed and worry about covering for yourself. You have to understand what's going on. The devil is after the gift. Here's the deal: that's why he's been trying to kill you. Because you knew all your life you were gifted. You knew it. You'd be in crowds of people and you'd go hang out and you knew that wasn't really you. Because you knew there was something different and unique about you. You've known for some time that you were gifted. You've known it. And the reality is that the devil cannot take the gift, because he cannot take what he did not give. For him to take the gift would make him greater than the Giver of the gift. Because every good

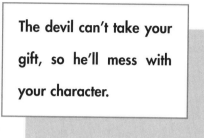

The devil can't take your gift, so he'll mess with your character.

and perfect gift comes from above—it comes from God. So the devil knows he cannot take the gift, but he tries anyway. Because he cannot take the gift, what he will try to do is contaminate your character. If he can contaminate your character, it will derail the glory that the gift brings.

He can't get your voice, that's a gift, but he'll mess with your character. Gifted character can be contaminated and the very gift that God gives not be manifested to the glory of God. What the devil wants to do is to turn the gift back on you. So he says, "I know you're gifted and I can't touch the gift. But I'll mess you up in your flesh so bad that when you do operate in the gift the glory will come back to you." And if the glory comes back to you it's not going to go to God because the rule of engagement is that God's not going to share His glory with anybody! That's why the devil's like, "Go on and sing, go on and do your thing, go and work," because he knows it's all about you! That's why the devil's trying to get you, he's trying to mess with your character; he's trying to taint your testimony. It doesn't matter how gifted you are, he can mess you up.

Paul tells Timothy, "Don't be ashamed of your testimony because where you've been can keep you grounded." Because where you've been is your testimony. God brought you from a mighty long way. You realize that you don't have time to get beside yourself because whatever God does through you is not for you, but it's for His glory.

So the trial is necessary; the persecution becomes necessary, because the persecution is an affirmation. Without the persecution, I wouldn't be affirmed that I'm a threat to the devil's kingdom. The gift is a threat to his kingdom, so he has to attack me; if he's not attacking me, I'm not a threat. If you're going through attack, you ought to shout because you got the devil nervous.

YOU ARE SAVED FOR THIS MOMENT

Paul goes on to tell Timothy to endure difficulties like a good soldier; stop whining, man, you're on the battlefield. You have got to understand who you are, and the only way God's gonna get the glory is that you persevere. In 1 Timothy 4:9-10, we're taught, "You are saved for this moment." God didn't save you to sit. God didn't go to Calvary for you to tell Him how rough it was and for you to give up. He said, "On Calvary you saw me **hanging** there; why can't you **hang in** there?" There are too many people sitting on it. But God is saying, "It's time to get up." People are always making excuses why they can't be the man or woman God wants them to be. It's time for us to say, "Lord, whatever you do through my life, I'm gonna make sure I give you the glory!"

> **Jesus hung on there on the cross, so you can hang in here.**

When somebody makes an investment, when the investor makes an investment, he has to believe in that investment. He has to say, even while looking at his falling investment, that I am not going to bother it; because I believe that even though it's hit rock bottom, it's gonna come back. When

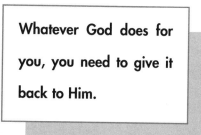

Whatever God does for you, you need to give it back to Him.

God made an investment in you—this is what Calvary was about—you had hit rock bottom. God could've said, "I'm gonna take you back—no, I'm gonna kill you because you know you messed up," but God said, "I just have to wait. That investment is gonna turn around and that investment is gonna come from rock bottom and that investment is gonna eventually be where I want it to be." God believes enough in me to give me another chance to get my stuff together, that's why I don't have time to sit on it. For everything God's done in my life I'm gonna make certain that God gets the glory.

Whatever God does in your life, you ought to give it back to Him. God gives you a job, you ought to give it back to Him. You ought to do it to the glory of God. If God has called you to preach, preach to the glory of God. If God has called you to teach, teach to the glory of God. If God has called you to be a mechanic, do it to the glory of God. And when you do it to the glory of God, God will be glorified.

WHEN GOD IS GLORIFIED, HE EDIFIES ME

When God is glorified, then the person that gave it to God is edified. In other words, when I lift God up, God turns right back around and lifts me up. When I glorify God, what I'm saying is, "Lord, thank you." And what God is saying when He edifies me is, "You're welcome." When God is glorified, then I'm edified, and all of my needs are satisfied. I don't have to worry about how this gift is going to work, because God will make room. The Bible says, "Your gift will make room for you."

This means that God will satisfy your every need; and then once God satisfies me, my haters are going to look at me and they're gonna say, "How did you get what you've got when I know where you've been?" I'll look at them and say, "I'm justified because had it not been for the grace of God I wouldn't be here today. God's been glorified, I've been **edified**, my needs have been **satisfied**, because I've been **justified**."

Don't sit on it. When you look back over your life and see how far God has brought you, how can you **not** give God the glory? How can you not give God the praise?

There is greatness on you. You are from a generation of greatness. All of us have some special folk in our family. (I know somebody will say, "My family was jacked up, Bishop. I know what you're talking about because my family wasn't all that great.") All of us have some jacked-up family members—the crazy uncles and incredible cousins—but there was somebody you could look to and say, "Hey, Lord, please let that pass down."

There's a decision you have to make in your life. Don't sit on it. Move with it. "Lord, work on me that I don't pass down a curse to the next generation. I want to pass down a blessing. Lord help me tap into the gift that you've given me." As a couple pray, "Lord, work on us so we can pass a blessing to the next generation. Help us glorify you as we keep our date with destiny."

WHOSE ARE YOU AS A COUPLE?

1. What is your favorite excuse?
2. Who have been your mentors? a coach? a pastor? a co-worker? a boss? a family member? As a couple, talk about your mentors and decide if you need a couple mentor.
3. How can you help each other make better choices?
4. Quietly listen to each other as you talk about what you think God is calling you to do.
5. On a scale from one to ten (one being low and ten being high), how likely are you to procrastinate?
6. Do you regularly put things off that you need to get done? What will help you move on?
7. Talk to each other about your family of origin. Who were the spiritual leaders? Who prayed for you? What were you taught about church? Who is the spiritual leader in your house now?
8. Who looks up to you? How can you be a better example?
9. How do you want to bless the next generation? What things do you want to pass down?
10. How do you think your children or other family members see you as a couple? as individuals?
11. Do something to celebrate your life as a couple.

CHAPTER SIX

WALK IN DESTINY: GO FOR IT!

When we move in God's purpose, God is **glorified**, we are **edified**, and the devil is **horrified**. But it hinges on our decision. We can choose to sit on it, but we know we need to move it and stir it up. And we can see that making that date with destiny means we pass our blessing to the next generation. There is something we must do.

In the Bible, Isaiah 6:1-8 says:

> In the year that King Uzziah died I saw also the Lord sitting upon a throne, high and lifted up, and his train filled the temple. Above it stood the seraphims: each one had six wings; [with two] he covered his face, and [with two] he covered his feet, and [with two] he did fly. And one cried unto another, and said, "Holy, holy, holy, is the LORD of hosts: the whole earth is full of his glory." And the posts of the door moved at the voice of him that cried, and the house was filled with smoke. Then said I, Woe is me! for I am undone; because I am a man of unclean lips, and I dwell in the midst of a people of unclean lips: for mine eyes have seen the King, the LORD of

hosts. Then flew one of the seraphims unto me, having a live coal in his hand, which he had taken with the tongs from off the altar: And he laid it upon my mouth, and said, Lo, this hath touched thy lips; and thine iniquity is taken away, and thy sin purged. Also I heard the voice of the Lord, saying, Whom shall I send, and who will go for us? Then said I, Here am I; send me.

There is something that God has ordained for your life. And regardless of your present circumstances, there is a mandate upon your life to fulfill the will of God in the earthly realm that you might bring glory to His name. The truth is that it really doesn't matter what people feel about you—how they view you. You have to realize that whenever God gets ready to use a person He has a way of propelling them beyond the witness of their past into the promise of their future. It really doesn't matter what mistakes you've made, how colorful your personal biography may be; when God says He's ready to use you, you got to get up and do what God says do.

But you say, "Walker, man, I want to walk in God's purpose. I'm motivated to move on it and stir it up, but . . ." And that's where I want you to stop. Stop with the word "but," because you've got to realize that God don't take excuses; there is no time for delay. You must say to yourself: "It's time for me to do what God is calling me to do; there is an encounter awaiting me; there is a great experience awaiting me; and you, Brother Walker, have to declare that there is something I

> **When God uses you, He can propel you into the promise of your future.**

must do." I know people may not understand it, but you've got to realize this is about your destiny; this is about your future. And you've got to make up in your mind that you're not going to let anything or anybody prevent you from doing what God calls you to do.

The prophet Isaiah is experiencing his call into ministry. God calls Isaiah through a series of personal experiences with God. Maybe like Isaiah, you've experienced God. Maybe you're not sure. But when God says He's ready for you to step out, you've got to move out of your agenda. There has to be something inside of you that declares, "No matter what happens, I'm going to do what God told me to do." So what do you do? Where do you get the power to face down those obstacles life throws at you?

GOD GIVES US A POWERFUL REVELATION OF HIMSELF

When God calls us into destiny and God calls us into purpose, we have to acknowledge God's power. Let me break it down: whenever God gets ready to use us, He always gives us a revelation of Himself to confirm His request. Too many people find it easy to say, "God told me," which only means that they heard what they wanted to hear. Maybe God said that and maybe He didn't. When God calls you, He will also send you confirmation. When you think you hear God talking to you, it's a good idea to talk

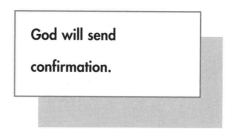

God will send confirmation.

> **Be clear about the "who," so you don't have to ask "how?"**

about it with your mentor or with a small, reliable group of Christian friends.

So whenever God gets ready to use you, you will always get a greater revelation of who God is.

Why is this significant? **We have to be clear about the "who," so we will not have to ask "how."** God says to an eighty-something Moses, "Tell Pharaoh to let my people go." Moses, with only a stick and a stutter, asks, "How am I going to do that?" And God reminds him, "Don't you know who I am? *I Am That I Am* is sending you. When you get there, I am already there."

Somebody right now reading this book is trying to figure out how are you gonna do what God told you to do. But don't you know He is the *I Am?* You're trying to figure out how the bills are going to get paid, He says, "*I Am.*" You're trying to figure out who's gonna open up the door, He says, "*I Am.*" You're trying to figure out how in the world a way is gonna be made? He says, "*I Am.*" You're trying to figure out, "How am I gonna deal with all these haters?" He says, "*I Am.*"

GOD HAS A STRATEGY

Once you get a revelation of *who* God is, then it moves you into the service of the Lord. Whenever God begins to move us into destiny, God always moves strategically in time and space, because God plans ahead about how He moves. That's why you have to realize that whatever He does He has a divine timing. He could have sent Jesus at any time throughout history, but the scripture says, "When the fullness of time had come, God sent

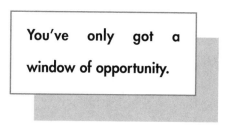

You've only got a window of opportunity.

forth His son, made of a woman." In other words, you have to realize that whenever God calls, He says, "I'm calling you at a *specific time.* There is only a *window of time* in which you have to move." And when God calls you forth, you're gonna have to step through that window and do what God says.

The Isaiah passage is interesting because it happened in the year that King Uzziah died. Who was King Uzziah? King Uzziah was a great king: he had position, he had prominence, he had power, he had influence. I mean, King Uzziah, he comes to the throne at age fifteen; he reigns fifty years; I mean, King Uzziah had influence. He had popularity; he had prestige; when you think about authority, you are thinking about King Uzziah. When you think about power, you are thinking about King Uzziah. And you have to understand what the problem is; it was only *after* King Uzziah's death that Isaiah experienced the presence of the Lord.

I don't know what's got influence in your life, but God says, "I'm getting ready to allow some stuff to die in your past, so that you can finally seek God for yourself." There's some relationships, there's some things, that have had too much influence over you. And it's got to die so that you can have a personal encounter with God for yourself.

So when Uzziah died, you've got to realize that God was trying to show Isaiah who was really in control, who really had the power, who really had the prestige. God is saying to Isaiah, what you're getting ready to go into, Uzziah can't help you. You're gonna need to know who's really in control. So the Bible says that Isaiah looked up and "saw the Lord . . . high and lifted up, and his train filled the temple." Now, you have to understand that the people measured a king's might and power by the length of his train. They would put the train on like a cape, and it would drape behind the king. If it was a small train, his kingdom was small; if it was a long train, his kingdom was huge. King Uzziah had a major train because he had a lot of territory, a lot of land. His train probably could fill a whole room. But when Isaiah saw God "high and lifted up," His train not only filled the room, it filled the whole house.

God gave Isaiah a powerful revelation of Himself to prove that He is in control, that everywhere Isaiah could go, God's in control. God knows that we need to have reassurance. He knows how hard it is for us to step out in faith. He knows how hard it is for us to trust in things we can't see. He's not God for nothing. He knows you're scared; He knows your weaknesses and strengths. He knows it all and he chooses you anyway and perhaps because of them.

YOU GOT TO HAVE THE SONG

In Isaiah the Scripture reveals three important things. The first is that the seraphim came and they sang in unison, "Holy, holy, holy." Whenever you see the Lord's power, you have to have a song. There are two kinds of angels: there are cherubim and seraphim. Cherubim are warrior angels. These were the angels that God put in the garden after He threw out Adam and Eve. But seraphim are ministering angels; they worship—they worship Him who sits upon the throne. And the Bible said that they all sang in unison, "Holy, holy, holy."

When you meet God for yourself and you see God's power, you got to get that song. Your soul has got to know that song. You know what holy really means? Holy is a worship song. Here are some of the lyrics: God, this is not contingent upon what You do for me, this is contingent upon who You are. So God, if You don't heal my body, You're still holy. If I don't get the job, You're still holy. If You don't work the situation out, You are still holy. You've got to make up in your mind. You see, the children of Israel missed this in Psalm 137 after they had been taken captive by the Babylonians and the Babylonians wanted them to sing a song. And they said, "How shall we sing the Lord's song in a strange land?" It's because they forgot that your song is not about what God does for you, but it's about who God is.

When you know who God is, you can be like Paul and Silas (Acts 16:25). It may be midnight and you may be in prison, but you can give God praise right there. Every now and then you've got to say, "Lord, You're just holy. Lord, you don't have to do any-thing else for me, You're just holy. God, if you don't do nothing else, You've already done enough. You're just holy."

FOUNDATIONS WILL SHIFT

And I want you to understand some-thing; I want you to get this second

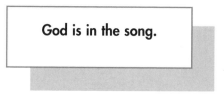

God is in the song.

> **The blessing you've been waiting on is too big for a little door.**

thing. Not only was there a song but there was also an earthquake, so violent that the foundations were shaken and the doors flew open. God's power was in the earthquake. Whenever you serve God, God says, "I'm moving in the supernatural to rearrange things in the natural." Whenever you are walking in purpose, God says, "I'm gonna shake some things up." God says, "I'm gonna take the thing you've been leaning on, the person you've been depending on for access. And now you're not going to have to kiss anybody's behind; you're not going to have to run up behind anyone, because," God says, "I'm gonna rip the doorposts off and give you unlimited access. As a matter of fact, the blessing that you've been waiting on is too big for the little door anyway."

GOD'S POWER IS LIKE SMOKE

Third, you can see God's power in the smoke. Not only was there a song and a shifting, but the Bible says in Isaiah 6:4, "The house was filled with smoke." Whenever you want to see the power of God, you've got to see it in the smoke. Smoke is symbolic of the very power and the presence of God. Smoke filled the house. And you know what smoke does; it does three things.

- First, smoke chokes out everything that isn't supposed to be in it. You've got to understand this about the presence of God: God says, "I'm gonna choke out everything that isn't right." That's why you don't have to be mean to people who don't like you; you don't have to cuss them out; all you have to do is just worship on your job and watch how God will choke some people out of your life. Some people are making you crazy, and God says, "I'm gonna choke them out. All you have to do is just worship me."

- Second, not only does smoke choke, it also ascends, it rises. And God says, "Whenever you have My presence, your low places are over now. You can't hang out with low people going nowhere."

- And third, if you know anything about smoke, you know that whenever a person has been in smoke, smoke gets in the hair, it gets in the clothes; and I don't care how much you try to wash it off, it's going to be a few days before the smoke goes away. Whenever you've been in the presence of God, we can tell 'cause you smell like smoke—you look like smoke. Being in God's presence leaves its scent on you.

SEE YOURSELF FOR WHO YOU REALLY ARE

When Isaiah sees God high and lifted up, the seraphim singing, he sees God's train, and sees the smoke, Isaiah gets convicted. In verse 5 he says, "Then said I, 'Woe is me.'" I am messed up. I'm not buying anything. I'm a man of unclean lips, and everybody around me is just like me. When I'm in the presence of the Holy One, I can't help seeing how unholy, how unlike God I am. Whenever you walk in purpose, you see God; the next thing you're gonna see is who you really are. That's why people who walk in purpose are not judgmental, because

But I'm only me, Lord.

how am I gonna judge you when I see myself and I know I've done wrong?

There is an old story that says that the hardest thing for a person to do is look into the mirror and see what is really there. Even if it is difficult for us to see ourselves as we truly are, we still need to see our path and see ourselves walking on it. This leads us to worship, and worship makes you transparent and humble. It helps you see things the way they truly are.

One thing that we need to see is that we were originally intended to be in the image of God. Not only that, but other people who walk in purpose are also intended to be in the image of God. This means you and **all** Christians. What the devil tries to do is distort the very image that God originally intended for my life. And so he put these image-nations—the way the nations view my image in my head. And so I thought that I had to have my house a certain way, I thought I had to have my eyes a certain color, I thought I had to have the right size in this and the right this and that.

When you understand the image of God, you see that you're **not** defined by the nations, but that you **are** defined by God. You can declare, "If God made my head big, so what! If God made my lips this way, He wanted them that way. He made my hips like He wanted my hips. And if you have a problem with it, you can take it up with the Creator. You go your way and I'm going my way, and may the Lord watch between us while we're apart. Because I'm not defined by what you say; I'm in the image of God."

SEE YOURSELF THROUGH GOD'S EYES

When Isaiah saw the Lord, Isaiah saw himself for who he was with all his issues, but God saw Isaiah as he was too. Yet God decided to use him because God knew Isaiah's destiny. Let me tell you something, I know how people are and you do too. You know people are a little judgmental sometimes, because they look and compare themselves with other people.

Sometimes people are just hard on themselves: "How can God use me with all the stuff I've done?" Let me tell you something, when I was in high school and I was in twelfth grade, I had a car. My dad let me have an old Subaru. Boy, it was bad. I loved that car. You know when you're in the twelfth grade and you have car, you have it going on. So there I was with a car in the twelfth grade—I had it going on—until I wrecked it. When I wrecked that car, my daddy made me keep driving it. Fender was falling off; it was all ugly at that point. I would try to park it in the back and kids would come around and talk about my car because it was a disaster. It was wrecked, but I was still driving it. You know what my daddy said? "Boy, keep driving it. Let people talk about it, keep driving it. Ain't nothing wrong with the engine." I may be a wreck, but greater is He that is in me than he that is in the world. And every time I keep coming to church, God keeps getting the stuff out of me. He keeps straightening me up. He keeps getting the bumps and bruises out. God sees you as you are, but He also sees who you can become.

THE ASSIGNMENT RELEASES YOUR POTENTIAL

Your assignment releases your potential. This is important because just as Isaiah realizes how God taps into this incredible

> **God sees the good stuff in you that nobody else sees.**

potential inside of him, God sees stuff in you that nobody else sees. You've got to stop making excuses as to why you can't do what God wants you to do. I mean, I know you're not perfect and I know you made some mistakes, but you've got to know how to put stuff in your past. It's time to go for it.

You have to understand that God consecrated Isaiah for his assignment. The Bible says in verses 6 and 7, after Isaiah has a pity-party in verse 5 about his own inadequacies (my paraphrase), "One of the seraphim flew and it had a live coal in his hand he took out of the fire." A live coal, it was on fire, and he put it on his mouth. That had to be painful, "and he put it on his mouth and he said to him 'This [coal] hath touched your lips and your iniquity is taken away and your sin has been purged.'" In other words, sometimes pain is necessary to get you to purpose. Sometimes you have to go through some pain. But this pain is necessary to get some things out of you, to get your attention, so that you can get to where God's trying to take you.

PURIFIED BY FIRE

God consecrated Isaiah. That means that God set him apart for purpose and this consecration always involves fire. And fire symbolizes three things: light, heat, and purification.

- First: **light**. Whenever you see fire, you will always, always have light. Light is where revelation or knowledge dawns.

When you say about a person that the "light came on," or a "light bulb came on in their head," that's what you're saying. They got an idea, some inspiration, or some new knowledge. God says, "When I consecrate you, I do not consecrate ignorance but I consecrate revelation. I have to build you up in the Word of the Lord because I'm not gonna send you out somewhere ignorant." Why would you send a fireman out who didn't know how to put out a fire? Why would you send a policeman out that didn't know how to use his gun? You have to equip the saints for the work of ministry, which is revelation. God says, "The things I'm taking you through are preparing you for something you can't handle right now." That's called revelation.

• Second: **heat**. Not only does fire produce light, fire also brings heat. Heat represents the test that you have to go through. Because in 1 Peter 4:12 the Bible says, "Think it not strange concerning the fiery trial which is to try you." God says, "I can't use anyone who hasn't been through anything. You have to go through some tests, so that whenever I take you where I'm taking you, you can look back and tell somebody what you've been through, so that they can make it through the same thing you made it through." So bring on the heat.

• Third: **purification**. The fire also symbolizes purification. God says, "I'm a consuming fire and I'll burn out everything that ain't right in your life." God eliminates stuff in your life in order to purify you. God says, "Don't worry. There's gonna be a consuming fire that's gonna come and eliminate some things in your life." God purifies you so He can trust you with purpose.

And it's only after you've been through the light, the heat, and the purification by eliminating unwanted things in your life that God speaks. God didn't say anything until Isaiah went through all that. Some of you may be wondering why God isn't speaking to you. God says, "I'm not going to entrust this greatness to you, with you playing around. I have to take you through some stuff so that when I tell you what I want you to do, I know you're gonna do it. I don't have time to play with people. You don't know if you want to be in the world or in the church. I have to be sure. You're undecided? I'm not gonna trust this greatness to you unless I know you're gonna do what I'm telling you to do."

WHO WILL REPRESENT US?

And so you have to qualify for this call. God says, "Who shall I send? Who will go for us?" Us? What do you mean? Us? Who was us? I mean, you've got to understand something. You've got to understand that whenever God calls, He is asking for a representative. Who's gonna represent us? Us who? God the Father, God the Son, and God the Holy Ghost. In other words, God the Father says, "Who's gonna represent us? Who's going for us? I mean, who's gonna go, and who's gonna allow me to be Lord over their life and control them? Who's gonna walk in integrity with the Word? Who's gonna walk in the Spirit? Who's gonna be led by the Spirit?" I know some people that go, but they go for themselves. They go for their own agenda; they go for popularity; they go for the check; they go because they want people to pat them on the back; they go because their self-esteem is so low they just need somebody to smile at them.

But God says, "I'm trying to figure out who's gonna go for us? Who's gonna represent me wherever I take them?"

God will lead you through the fire.

God says, "If I give you prestige in your field, are you still going to represent us? I want to know if you're gonna still give us the glory?" You may have to walk through fire to get where God wants you to go. As a couple, you may have to endure hardship and grief, but a date with destiny is worth it.

ARE YOU READY?

There is a question of representation, but there is also a question of readiness. Because you've been talking about you being ready to go and God says, "Now I'm getting ready to release you into your assignment." There is something you have to do. You have to stop making excuses and get up off your blessed assurance and you have to do what God says do.

This is serious business, so you'd better be talking about it as a couple. Walking together in purpose means conferring, talking things over, and, yes, sharing your feelings about what's happening to you both. When you're a couple walking in purpose, if something happens to one of you, it happens to the other—it happens to both of you.

Walking together in purpose means talking things over.

The Bible talks about marriage partners being equally yoked. Back in Jesus' day, they used oxen to plow the fields. And let's say that one ox could pull two tons and the other ox could pull six tons. Do you know how many tons they could pull as a team? Twelve tons! As individuals, you can only take so much, walk so far, work so hard; but as a couple working side by side, you, together, can do so much more. As individuals you are priceless to God, but as a team, you're worth even more.

HERE I AM; SEND ME

Isaiah teaches us that it's one thing to be called, but it's another thing to answer the call. He says, "Here am I; send me." *Here am I* is an affirmation of responsibility. *Here am I* says, "Lord, I realize that you are talking to me and not somebody else." *Here am I* says, "Lord, regardless of what I had planned, regardless of my agenda, I'm ready to do what you want me to do." This is what Moses said when God said, "Moses, Moses." Moses says, "Here am I." *Here am I* says, "It doesn't make a difference what I had on my little agenda or my schedule, God, I make you my schedule and my agenda."

We need some *Here am I* people in the house of God. Not use-somebody-else-God or not always-there-they-are-God or they'll give or they'll show up so what difference does it matter if I show up? We need some folk that can declare, "Lord, I want to be in position to receive what you have for my life. And God, if nobody else will get in position, Lord, here am I." If you need somebody to go the extra mile, here am I; send me. "God, if you need somebody to help somebody along the way, here am I. If you need somebody to tithe, here am I. If you need somebody on my pew to praise your name, here am I."

YOU ARE CHOSEN

And Isaiah discovered and I've come to proclaim over your life that you've been chosen. As you read this book, put it down and say to yourself, "I'm one of the chosen ones." God could've chosen anybody, but God chose you.

The Bible says, "Many are called but few are chosen." Do you know that there is a difference between those that are called and those that are chosen? To be called simply means that I answered the call, it means sometimes I only go when it's convenient to **me**. It means: I only go when things are easy for **me**. But when you are chosen, you will go when it's not convenient. When you are chosen, you will go even if they don't pay you to go. When you're chosen, you will go if nobody likes you. You will go even if you make enemies; you will go and do what God wants you to do.

It's time for some people to do what God told us to do, but there are three main reasons why people don't do what He told them to do.

- The first reason is that some people are **fatigued**. They may say, "Lord, I would do what You want me to do, but I'm so tired." And God says, "The reason why you're tired is because you got so much disorder in your personal life that when it comes to the things of God, you're always worn down." But God says, "If you get those crazy folk out of your life and you stop running in those crazy places, you won't be so tired. And you'll have strength to do what I want you to do."

Isaiah discovered this later on in Isaiah chapter 40:28-31. He says, "Hast thou not known? hast thou not heard, that the everlasting God, the LORD, the Creator of the ends of the earth, fainteth not, neither is weary? there is no searching of his understanding. **He giveth power** to the faint; and to them that have no might he increaseth strength." Then he adds, "Even the youths shall faint and be weary, and the young men shall utterly fall: but they that wait upon the LORD shall renew their strength; they shall mount up with wings as eagles; they shall run, and not be weary; and they shall walk, and not faint." If you go for it, God will give you power.

- But then somebody else says, "I would go but I'm so **frustrated**. The truth is, I hear what God wants me to do, but every time I take one step, the devil knocks me back three steps. Every time I look for support, nobody encourages me; all these people around me are trying to take me out." But I hear the Lord saying, "Be not weary in doing well but in due season." I'm here to tell you that your season is due now.

- Then somebody else says, "I would go but I'm too **fearful**. I've got a spirit of fear on my life. I'm afraid of what people gonna say; I'm afraid of getting out of my comfort zone; I'm afraid of what might happen." But let these words reassure you, "God has not given us the spirit of fear; but of power, and of love, and of a sound mind!" So go for it; make up your mind to do that thing that God has told you to do. Even if you have to go by yourself, if nobody understands, if people laugh at ya, say, "I'm gonna do what God told me to do."

Jesus didn't get up for you to sit down. But when He got up, He said, "All power is in My hands." And He said, "Go there-

Jesus didn't get up for you to sit down.

Jesus didn't get up for you to sit down.

fore into all the earth and teach them, baptizing them in the name of the Father, and of the Son, and of the Holy Ghost. And where you go, I'll be also." Say to yourself, "Where I go He walks with me, He talks with me. He tells me that I am His own." I don't know about you, but I'm packing my bags, I'm getting my stuff together, I'm getting ready to do what God wants me to do. God is looking for somebody that's ready to step out of their comfort zone and say, "I'm going to where God wants me to go." I'm gonna press my way through my tears, I'm gonna press my way through criticism because I want to hear Him say, "Thou good and faithful servant, you've been faithful over a few things. Come on up, I'm gonna make you a ruler!" Go for something, there's something for you. Say to yourself, "Something I gotta do."

You've got something to do as an individual, but you've also got something to do as a couple. God has put you on a team. Many couples discuss the wonderful things that they want to do together, but until you begin to make concrete plans, you will be talking about it for years. Think about it. God brought you together as a couple to accomplish something in the earthly realm. Something big. Something that will change the world in which you live. All the gifts, resources, and vision that God has given to both of you cannot sit idle.

I have some dear friends who are high profile. I won't mention their names; however, it has been a joy for me to watch them move toward their destiny together. One day, they just woke up and realized that if they didn't do it, it wasn't going to get done. They had a million reasons why they hadn't done it—schedules, family commitments, and so forth. But they decided to make their relationship a priority, and they have developed one of the most powerful nonprofit organizations today. They realized the importance of prioritizing those things that matter in life.

All of us run and run, but the question is: Are we running the right race? Are we running in the right direction, chasing our destiny, or are we are fatigued because we are not fulfilling the assignments God has given us to achieve. It's time for you and your significant other to do this. Whatever it is, the world is waiting on you.

Go for it!

WALKING IN DESTINY AS A COUPLE

1. Share with each other a time when you saw or felt God moving in your life.

2. Every person carries a picture of God in their heads. What is your picture of God? What does that image say about who you believe God is?

3. What are some ways you'd like to serve God?

4. Talk about a time when you were chosen: for a team, for an assignment, for a job, for a date, for an honor, and so on. Who chose you and why?

5. What are some things that need to shift in your life? Are there some things you'd like to do differently as a couple?

6. What song do you carry in your heart? What kind of song is it? Happy? Sad? Angry? Fearful? Guilty? Ashamed? Proud?

7. Make a list of your best qualities. Make a list of your partner's best qualities.

8. Tell your partner one thing that you really love about them.

9. What kind of representative would you make for God? What are some situations where you believe that God could use you?

10. On a scale of one to ten (one being low and ten being high), how willing are you to go where God sends you?

CHAPTER SEVEN

A DATE FOR DESTINY: TOO DEEP FOR SHALLOW WATERS

My prayer for you as we come to the end of this book is that you've decided to meet your date with destiny, that you've decided to walk in purpose, and that you have a better understanding of the call God has placed on your life as an individual and as a couple. I hope that you've read the *Date with Destiny Forty Days Devotional* as a couple. I pray that your home is a haven of peace and blessing that you are passing to the next generation.

Maybe you've made mistakes like everybody. Maybe you've endured persecution and oppression. Maybe you've lost much and suffered, even suffered for the Lord. God is reaching out to you with His love and compassion. He's saying that it's never too late to start walking in purpose. God's hand is upon you to redeem, guide, comfort, inform, reveal, sustain, and heal. But God wants you to stay in the pressure and trust that He will use you to His glory and your true purpose. God is not out to "get" you, but he does need you to listen and move when He says move, go where He leads, and learn His ways.

> **It's never too late to start walking in purpose.**

But even with all the encouragement, knowledge, and decision possible, there comes a time when you have to go for it. There comes a time when you have to move and push out into the deep waters.

I remember when Stephaine and I were courting. She was doing extremely well at Harvard, but I knew if we were going to take this to the next level, preparations would have to be made for her transition to Nashville. When I brought up the subject of looking for a job in Nashville, you can only imagine the anxiety she felt. I had not proposed, so she had no guarantees other than my word. I saw her step into the deep and ready her vitae in preparation for pursuing employment in Nashville. She believed in the God in me and was willing to come out of the shallow waters of comfort toward the deep of her destiny. Of course, I did propose to her prior to her actually sending the résumé, but the fact that she began preparing it was enough proof that she was willing to partner with me in destiny. It takes faith to step out like that. I'm not telling you to make unwise decisions and walk away from your job because you love someone. I'm saying that you have to be willing to put yourself in position for God to do the rest.

You can practice and prepare all you want, but there comes a time when you have to do it. I once knew a young woman who wanted more than anything to go scuba diving in the Gulf of Mexico. She practiced in the swimming pool, went to the local lake, even took a few lessons. Finally the day came when she left for the Gulf. But the one thing she hadn't anticipated was the serious sting of the saltwater when she opened her eyes underwater. It was bad. But she'd practiced enough to know what to do. Even so, being in the deep water was very different from being in the shallow water of the pool. All I'm saying is that, when you push out into the deep waters of your life, there will be surprises and things you couldn't expect and didn't anticipate, but to be a successful diver, you have to do it—you have to go deep. You have to trust your training.

The disciples had a similar experience in Luke chapter 5. Here the Bible says:

> And it came to pass, that, as the people pressed upon him to hear the word of God, he stood by the lake of Gennesaret, and saw two ships standing by the lake: but the fisherman were gone out of them, and were washing their nets. And he entered into one of the ships, which was Simon's, and prayed him that he would thrust out a little from the land. And he sat down, and taught the people out of the ship. Now when he had left speaking, he said unto Simon, Launch out into the deep, and let down your nets for a draught. And Simon answering said unto him, Master, we have toiled all the night, and have taken nothing: nevertheless at thy word I will let down the net. And when they had this done, they enclosed a great multitude of fishes: and their net brake. And they beckoned unto their partners, which were in the other ship, that they should come and help them. And they came, and filled both the ships, so that they began to sink. When Simon Peter saw it, he fell down at Jesus' knees, saying, Depart from me; for I am a sinful man, O Lord. For he was astonished, and all that were with him, at the draught of the fishes which they had taken. (Luke 5:1-9)

PUSH YOUR LIMITS

There are things in our lives that require us to move beyond the comfort of our present environment. It has been said that if you want different results you have to do things differently. The fool literally continues to do the same thing over and over again expecting different results. You have to make a change. Perhaps you are a person who knows within yourself that the nature and the quality of what you desire far exceeds the very boundaries that enclose you. As a matter of fact, what you are after is pushing you, is pushing your limits, it's pushing you beyond your own boundaries.

It's easy to become content, however, to just be satisfied where you are. There are a lot of people who are just satisfied; they're content with the fact that things are just going to be the way they are. But when you recognize who you are and who you belong to, then it doesn't take long before you begin to realize that what you are after is in deep water.

You see, shallow water, the easy way, represents what everybody else is after; it really doesn't require much skill or much commitment. It doesn't really require any effort to wallow in shallow water. But when you're after something bigger and better for your life, your commitment has to go to another level. You see, this is

If you want different results, you have to do things differently.

what has happened in the Bible passage above. The disciples had gone fishing, and the Bible tells us they had caught nothing but frustration. They were washing their nets and about to give up, saying it's over. Jesus notices this and gets into their ships so He can better teach the crowd on the shore. When He has finished His teaching,

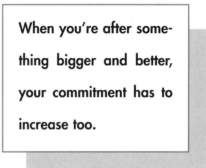

When you're after something bigger and better, your commitment has to increase too.

Jesus says to Simon Peter, "Launch out into the deep. Go out a little farther." And the Bible declares to us that something awesome happened when they obeyed the voice of the Lord, when they acted upon what Jesus said to do.

What God has for you is too deep for shallow water; it's too rich and too compelling for a casual acquaintance. When my young friend dove into those deep Gulf waters, she also wasn't anticipating the beauty of the ocean. The colors were more vivid than anything she'd ever seen in *National Geographic* or on the Discovery channel. And it was this beauty that drew her back again and again. What God's got for you is beyond your imaginings. But you have to take a deep breath and dive in first.

STEP OUT OF THE SHALLOWS

And maybe the reason why you haven't received the blessing that you've really been praying for is because God will not release it into shallow water. You've got to step out of your comfort zone and move out a little farther and get away from some things that are just too shallow in order to receive what God has

> **Take a deep breath and dive in.**

for your life. Maybe you hang out with shallow people and have shallow conversations. Been there, done that. What I'm after is in the deep. I'm after something much greater that God has for my life.

Let me break it down for you. It's interesting because the Bible says that these disciples were literally worn down by their experience; they had been toiling all night long, fishing in Lake Gennesaret, otherwise known as the Sea of Galilee, also called Lake Tiberias. The Bible says that when Jesus saw them out of their boat, He got in the boat and began to teach and preach to them and the others on the shore.

There are some people that literally have given up on some situations. Perhaps you are one of them. But God's got a word for you, and the first thing you've got to do is overcome frustration and fatigue. You've got to overcome it, so let's be real about it now. Because it's important to get this: the disciples are tired and they are frustrated. It's one thing to be tired, but it's another thing to be frustrated on top of weariness. And when Jesus encounters these disciples they had been fishing **all night long**. They had worked their entire shift and the Bible says they had caught nothing. Maybe that is you—maybe you've been going at it for a long time now, going through a ritual of routine over and over, and you've been struggling hard to make a thing work. And the truth is that nothing is happening in your life.

ARE YOU WASHING YOUR NETS?

Personally, I don't care how spiritual you are, how many Bible verses you've got memorized; I don't care how long you've been in church, everybody is subject to what happened to these disciples. It was a spirit of resignation that came over them. They gave up. Let's be real, the Bible said they were washing their nets. Washing their nets meant that they had resigned; it meant that they had said, "There is nothing else we can do. There are no fish out here. I'm through trying."

There's some of you that have said, "Pastor, I'm gonna be real with *you*. I have given this as much as I can give and I'm washing my net. I have poured out and poured out to people who aren't pouring back into me and I've washed my nets. I've tried to make the marriage work, but now I've washed my nets. I've tried to go back to school, but I don't have any support; I'm washing my nets." But I've got good news for you: you cannot quit because of what it looks like on the front end. You have to know that God's got something awesome on the back end, because it ain't over till God says so.

I'LL TAKE YOU AT YOUR WORD

The Bible says that in the midst of the fishermen washing their nets, Jesus shows up and Jesus gives them this word, "You've got to return and go back." And I need

> It ain't over till God says so.

somebody to get this, because you can't stay here and mope around and allow yourself to be a victim, based on what your situation has become. You have to pick yourself up and be willing to go back and do what God has asked you to do. I know there are some people who have given up, but God told me to tell you, "You have to get up and you have to go and try something different." Jesus says, "Launch out into the deep." And notice what they said: "Lord, we tried this all night long, but at Your word, we'll go back."

You can say, "Pastor, I've tried three times to qualify for the loan and they haven't given me the loan. But at your word I'll go back and do it again. I've tried to make this thing work in my family, but it isn't working. But if Jesus says so, I'll go back. I know what the doctor said: It isn't going to work, you aren't gonna be healed. But Lord, at Your word I'll still go back and try again." There's power in God's word. "Lord, at Your word I know I can do all things through Christ who strengthens me. At your word I know how to be not weary in well doing, but in due season I'll reap if I faint not. I know at Your word how to count it all joy when I fall. I know Your word is good. I know I can take You at Your word."

I know at His word that weeping may endure for a night, but joy comes in the morning. At Your word You were wounded for my transgressions, and by Your stripes I'm already healed. At Your word You will provide, You will supply every last one of my needs according to Your riches in glory.

> **God knows it's rough, but take Him at His word.**

Whenever you are frustrated, whenever you are fatigued, the Lord shows up and He says to you, "I know it's rough, but can you take Me at My word?"

STRENGTHEN YOUR FAITH BY LAUNCHING OUT

When you launch out into the deep, you will fortify your faith. But it's also about your behavior. I mean, Jesus shares with them where the blessing is; now, you have to get this too. In the midst of the situation Jesus shows up and He gives them a revelation. The revelation is that what you've been doing in shallow water isn't working. And that seems so simple, doesn't it? But how many times have you had to talk to your friends and tell people you know, "What ya doing ain't working." You have to do something different. You have to launch into deeper waters.

Do you know what the deeper waters are? Because you can do the right thing in the wrong place. You see, that's why you've got to evaluate the people you hang around with. You've got to evaluate the places you go, because shallow people will delay your blessing; shallow places will delay your blessings. What faith requires is a corresponding action. Planning and talking are fine and have their place, but in the end you have to act.

And once you get this, you can either stay in shallow water or you can launch out into the deep. It's your decision, your choice. God is not gonna mess with your free will. He's never messed with free will. So He says now, "I lay before you choice. You make the decision and you take responsibility for the consequence." But don't hold God accountable for the consequence of your

> **Your choice: stay in shallow water or launch out into the deep.**

decision. Because God just laid before you the choice. Now, here's the deal: you can be frustrated, worn down, and beaten down by the process, or you can fortify your faith and you can build yourself up, so that you can declare, "I'm going into the deep to get what God has for my life."

DEEP WATER IS WHERE LIFE IS

The deep water is also living water. In John chapter 4, Jesus meets the woman at the well, and he asks her for a drink of water. Now, here is why we know Jesus had a sense of humor. Jesus asks her for a drink, and she reacts saying that it's really strange that he (a Jew) would ask her (a Samaritan, who Jews considered less than dogs) for water. For one thing, he'd have to touch something she's touched, and she was considered unclean, untouchable. But apparently, he doesn't care about that. Instead, he says that if she knew who was asking, she'd ask him for living water. What we don't see in the English is that in the language Jesus spoke (Aramaic), the words for living water and deep well water were the same. He's playing with her. That's why he says that with her water, she'll get thirsty again; but with his, she'll be satisfied forever. The deep water is living water. It's where life is. It's the water we all truly want.

GOING DEEP MEANS BEING DEVOTED

But how many people really go to the deep water? Let's find out if you're going. Because there are three things you gotta know about deep water. The first is, you're gonna have to be devoted, you're gonna have to have some devotion. Because let me tell you something: what deep water does—it causes you to have to commit. See, when you're in the shallow water, there's not much commitment. You can always step out. You can take it or leave it. But when you're going to the deep, that's the point of no return. Let me break it down. When you're in the swimming pool and you're in the shallow end, you're like, "I don't want to be here; I want to get out." But now when you dive into the deep end, you've got to swim or you're gonna die.

Committed people—that's what God is looking for. He's tired of all these wishy-washy people. That's what the shallow folk do: go to church when they want to go to church; live right when it's easy; tell the truth when there's nothing at stake. God says, "I'm looking for some folk who are after the deep blessing. Got tired of you always having someone on your arm one month and somebody else on your arm another month. Can't you make up your mind? Leave all that shallow stuff alone and come on and go in the deep."

GOING DEEP TAKES DISCIPLINE

Then there's the need for discipline. Discipline requires focus. What do you mean, Pastor? Discipline means that my focus has to be exclusively on God. What do you mean? In the shallow water there are a lot of people. So if I need help or I need advice,

I just ask my partner, my buddy, I ask my dog, I ask my friend, it's no problem. But now the further I get out in the deep, the fewer people are out here. Some of you are discovering that; you are asking, "Lord, why is my crowd getting smaller?" If you want to get the riffraff out of your life, just start having deep conversations with them. Some folk can't even handle a deep conversation: "What do you do? What's your name?"

GOING DEEP MEANS DETERMINATION

Then you got to have determination. Because determination means taking as long as it takes. Determination says, "I'm out here now. You guys can leave if you're busy, but I'm not leaving until I get what I came for. As a matter of fact, if you want to know why you can't persuade me to move, it's because I went through too much hell to get out here." And tell them, "And I'm not going back empty-handed."

Our God is too deep for shallow water! The deep water is where God hangs out. Believe me, you've got to overcome your frustration or your fatigue. You've got His word; He gives us a Word. He says, "I'll give you a word; its time to go back." You've got to fortify your faith. You've got to get to that point in your life where you say, "Lord, I got to step out on it, I got to be devoted, I got to be disciplined, I got to have determination." Don't be discouraged or disheartened. God's made available to you His Word, Christian friends, mentors, even books like this. The decision to push out into deep water may be yours alone, but your walk in purpose doesn't have to be. You don't have to go it alone; but if you find yourself alone, you can always count on God.

THERE IS FAVOR IN YOUR FUTURE

Please understand the power of obedience. Because you've got to understand that the Bible says that obedience is better than sacrifice. I've also learned in my own life that favor is better than money. When you obey God, He will extend to you divine favor that you can't explain. Every relationship of destiny is one of favor. It's one that has the hand of God upon it and the blessings of the Lord in its future. It doesn't mean you won't have struggles. What it does mean is that God will honor your obedience and grant you blessings unmeasured. A lot of people have money but no favor. I've seen how they act when the money is gone. Unfavorably. When God's favor is upon you, you can lose everything and stay together because you know His favor has given you things money can't buy. There is no substitute for obedience.

When you do what God says do, it positions you to receive what God has for your life. What's interesting in this story about the disciples is what started out as frustration, what started out as fatigue, ends up as favor. You need to know that there is favor for your life too.

And because the disciples were obedient to what the Lord said do, the Bible says that they went through a season of reaping. Verse 6 says, "And when they had this done, they enclosed a great multitude of fishes: and their net brake."

You may think that this sounds much too simple. But God laid this on my heart to tell you, because on the surface it just seems like a cute story about some men who went fishing and didn't catch anything and got some good advice about fishing, and went a little further out and found the fish. But what God is saying to us today is, Stop waiting on Him to bring you the blessing. **You**

got to go where the blessing is. You're sitting back waiting on the blessing to fall out the sky, but you've got to understand something. You've got to understand what God is saying in your life. Listen, it was the same lake! Which says to me that when they weren't catching anything, it didn't mean there weren't any fish in the lake, it just meant they weren't in the right place in the lake. You think if you move to California, your frustrations will disappear? Maybe God is saying, "Nothing's wrong with the lake you're in, it's just something wrong with where you are in the lake."

The Bible said that their nets were filled with fish; it looked like God navigated circumstances where fish started volunteering for the net. Say to yourself, "Blessings will be volunteering for me." It looked like fish started coming from Bass Boulevard, from Trout Trace, from Lobster Lane, from Salmon Street, and fish started jumping in the net. So walk in purpose and get ready for an unusual season of blessing. Talk about this as a couple. Know that God is blessing you, but you've got to move into the deep water and know that this is going to be the net-breaking season for you both.

And the Bible says that when Peter saw the multitude of fishes, Peter went down and Peter fell at Jesus' feet and he really said, "This is blowing my mind." When I think of the goodness of Jesus and all He's done for me, my soul cries Hallelujah! I thank God for saving me, and every time I turn around, He keeps on doing great things for me! It's too deep for shallow water.

Are you ready to meet your destiny? Are you

> **You got to go where the blessing is.**

ready to be molded and remade into what God desires for your life? Are you ready to be devoted, disciplined, and determined? Whether you are afraid, tired, or frustrated, God is there calling you, beckoning you to come join Him in the deep water.

GOING DEEP AS A COUPLE

1. What are your limits? Do you need to push beyond them? What is holding you back?

2. If life is like a swimming pool, do you live at the shallow end or at the deep end?

3. What do you think the disciples thought when Jesus told them to get back in the boat and put out into the deep water?

4. It's easy to say, "Trust God," but do you? On a scale from one to ten (one being low and ten being high), how much do you trust God?

5. Is there somewhere or someone in your life that you need to turn over to God?

6. Being in mission and ministry strengthens faith. Where would you like to be in mission and ministry?

7. On a scale from one to ten (one being low and ten being high), how devoted are you to your job, your church, your family, each other?

8. Where do you need more discipline in your life? Do you need help to keep you accountable? If so, who can help?

9. On a scale from one to ten (one being low and ten being high), how determined are you to live a godly life?

10. Share with each other where God is calling you.

11. If you have God's assurance of success, what do you need to do differently?

12. Celebrate the blessings that God is giving you.

13. As a couple, what are you doing now that is taking you into the deep water?